MW00880300

A NEW FIRE IN YOU

Table of Contents

1

Acknowledgements

This book is dedicated to my deceased father, Frederick Mercer. My father gave 23 years of his life defending his beloved country, the United States of America, by serving in the United States Army, which I believe is the ultimate act of love and sacrifice. He also inspired hundreds of youth in the community of Chicago Heights, Illinois (*a small suburban community south of Chicago*) through his participation in countless volunteer events over many years. Thanks also to my mother, Elizabeth Mercer, who is the true backbone of our family. A very special thank you to my friend, the Author, Henry Abraham, who inspired me to "*Go for it*" and keep on writing. Shouts go out to my entire supporting cast of family and friends who helped me climb to the top and encouraged me through my troublesome times. These people are so vitally important to me that I felt compelled to mention them by name. My siblings: Fred, Mike, Chris and Robin. My relatives: Alexis and Nick Armbruster; Kathy and James Thornton; Rose Kavnaugh; Jutta,

Marcus, Betina, and Freddy Mercer; Laura, Michelle, and Lizzy Mercer. The Burney family; Richard and Mary Mercer; Virginia (Aunt Tootsie) Mercer; Tom and Gerri Mercer; The Rachman family; The Sandoval-Reynoos family; The Dominisky family; The Price family; The Stewart family; The Williams and Hodges families; the Mealing family; and the Aramil family.

Thanks also to Dr. Lenny Robinson and family. Travis Lathem, Ernest and Sevena Davis, Sandy Stoll, Karen Koch, Maria Quintinella (Rookie), the Phillip family, Karen De'Quir, Ken Nash, Dennis Lung, John Joyce, Chuck Saby, Joe Butler, George Gray, Dave and Debbie Carrier, The Bauer family, George Egoske and son Mark, Billy Yarbourogh, Patrick Kelly, Reyonous Burnette, Sir Vino Lemon, Dr. Jones, Mr. Burnett, Mr. McDaniels, Ron Grace. The Blinds family, Mick and Mary Kahills,. The Conte Family, Herb Fergason, Everette Khols,. The Lanes Family, the McClinton Family, The Austin and Johnson Family. Blair Benedict, Dr. Roger Marshall, Andre Dixon and The Hudspeth Family. The Staniceks, The Macy's, The Vanslykes, The Lombardis Family, Tim Hardimans, Roy

Scott, Ken Kahill, Ray and Larry McCoy, The Blackmans, Rich Township High Schools of Illinois. The Clarks, Rob and Tammy Moroney, Aaron Robinson, The Switzers family, Rocky Hill, Phillip Gary, the Will Family, Martin Horn, the Luscious Family. Neil and Family, Allen Greenberg, Cheryl Hudson, Amy Apke, Linda Ferguson, Karen Riddick, Gregg White-Bloom, Nadene Wright, Robin Pierce, Nan Williams, Suni Patel. The Blackwood family, The Gengos family, Kim Green, and the Jackson family.

Thank you to all of my basketball homies in the south suburbs of Chicago, my Kansas State University Wildcats Track and Field Teammates, the entire staff of Circle Family Services who helped keep me spiritually, physically and mentally rooted and on the right path, the staff of Cook County Illinois Correctional Facility and Counseling Service, The Chicago Dough Company of Richton Park, Illinois, The Park Forest Police Department, Threshold's Faculty and Staff – Bridgewest location, Larry Lehman of Liberty Tax Services-Oak Lawn, Illinois, Bob and his Seven-Eleven Store of Park Forest,

Illinois, and Mike Jennings of ON U the Signature Statement-onunation.com.

Thanks to all of the wonderful food pantries and churches that assisted me without prejudice or judgment, but encouraged me to do better and become a better person.

There are certainly an enormous amount of people who have befriended, assisted and corrected me. There are so very many people and supportive services that I may not have mentioned, but for whom my love and appreciation is just as deep.

Miller's Prediction

These thoughts were shared by Miller in the 1983 Kansas State University – Royal Purple Yearbook...Text from page 246.

*"Their intensity is much greater simply because of the idea of the Olympic Games — you see people in a different setting; one that you've never seen before," Miller said. Because of the competitiveness, Miller believes that K-State will have its share of athletes in the Games. "There are three to four people who have a shot at making it — Doug Lytle, Kelly Wenlock, Veryl Switzer and **Julius Mercer**. After those four, it will be a pretty tight race" Miller said. One of the people Miller feels strongly about is Mercer. Two years ago, Mercer was unknown in the Big Eight Conference. But, after last season's showing in the intermediate hurdles, winning the Big Eight outdoor and finishing high in the NCAA Indoor and Outdoor championships, Mercer has steadily become a known athlete. "Julius is going to*

have to run his lifetime best at the right time," Miller said of Mercer's chances in the trials.

Results: 1983 - at Stillwater, Oklahoma Olympic Trails.
Julius Mercer, 110 Hurdles - 13.79 1st place
Julius Mercer, 400 Hurdles - 51.03 1st place

Foreword

In February of 2009, a gentleman named Julius Mercer called and asked if I would be interested in assisting with the completion of his first book. We were brought together by a mutual friend, Anthony Mealing, who is the Physical Education Administrator-Director of Athletics at Aspira-Haugan Middle School in Chicago. Mealing has known Julius for over two decades and shared Julius Mercer's journey regarding his wonderful success in Track and Field, and what he has meant to the community of sports, education and life-skills development for people of all ages. Now Julius Mercer was writing his first book and asked me to collaborate with him to complete it. This task to me seemed not an effort, but a pleasure.

Every once in a while, a voice emerges from the depths of a man's soul that we have forgotten or chosen to ignore. This voice delivers words that ignite our consciousness and rekindles our sense of life's triumphs, challenges, struggles and precarious experiences. This book is *"keepin' it real"*; sometimes funny, often painful, but always full of metaphors and strategies for life *that work*. This book is a brilliant step toward enlightenment for people in any season of their lives, and it is reader friendly to all audiences.

This book is a close-up look into the incredible life of a man whose vulnerability is wounding, yet he has become a wiser man because of his personal testimony and professional growth. This book depicts a remarkable experience, exploding with honesty, courage, and determination of a man, who was also a world-class champion athlete. It is no surprised that he has taken to the task of exposing his life with such confidence and ease. After a few days into this project, I began to revisit snapshots of my youth in a country where crime, drugs, lack of jobs, single parent households, inefficiencies in education, the absence of positive moral and values, no spiritual or faith-based foundation, and every imaginable social ill can work to break the human spirit. Some youngsters rise above it but far too many fall victims to these elements. You won't reach the last pages of **"A New Fire in You"** without revisiting and resolving old issues, appreciating other people with a new love, seeing yourself in a whole new way and embracing this whole wonderful life that we have.

Julius Mercer has captured a unique way of helping others through his own transparency. This book offers a set of specific strategies he has utilized himself to rebound, recover, rejuvenate and re-strengthen his perspectives on life. I believe that this book is a must read for the student-athlete, the parents of student athletes, sports-athletic coaches, teenagers and teen-leadership counselors, youth ministers, recovery counselors, inmates, families of inmates, educational professional, business professionals, entrepreneurs and the list goes on. I'd like to think that this book stands as a testament to the potential in those individuals who are "behind the walls," "in the back of the class, in silence," "in the streets-with little hope," and be a source of encouragement and an awakening to

Americans everywhere to help a young person in your community to believe in the new American dream.

Michael A. Jennings, Chairman/CEO, ON U, Inc.

Creator of the logo driven signature statement… "it's on u"

Introduction

Hello, my name is Julius Mercer. Thank you for your generous contribution towards my Educational Seminars, Track and Field Clinics, and this book, which represents my experiences, triumphs, challenges, battles and promise to rise again and make a productive contribution toward the hope and future of Humanity.

I am a former graduate of Rich East High School and a resident of Park Forest, Illinois; a small, but beautiful community approximately thirty miles south of Chicago. I am known as a former world-class U.S. Track and Field Hurdler and one-time Olympic hopeful in 1984. I know firsthand what it is like to grow up having no aspirations. While in high school, I was an under achiever who managed to earn a GPA of 1.65. But through hard work, I became a proud graduate of Kansas State University and in 1966, I was inducted into the Kansas State University Athlete's Hall of Fame at Bramlage Fieldhouse. Shortly thereafter, an unexpected, untimely turn of events challenged my courage, the core of my spirit, and my very existence. Family crises had erupted all around me: my divorce and the death of my Father completely overwhelmed me and threw me into a cycle of severe depression, substance abuse, financial disaster, homelessness, mental institutions, near death experiences and then prison.

In March of 2007, as we say in track and field, "I gained my second wind." I decided to fully embrace this second opportunity in life to do something very positive and productive in order to assist my family, community, brothers and sisters as well as future generations. To that end I created a powerful motivational high school assembly program with live entertainment, geared toward the teenage crisis in America. The name of my project is **The UP-L.I.F.T. Project (Living Inspiration for Teenagers)**, which focuses on Empowering while creating a new awareness for teens that makes them think about themselves and life in a whole new way. It inspires them to feel a sincere sense of Love and Appreciation for others.

The **UP L.I.F.T. Project** has an almost instantaneous effect on a teenager's value system. It improves their academic successes, inspires them to increase their daily living responsibilities, and guides them to achieve their desired goals. The **UP L.I.F.T. Project** seeks out high school students who are failing to meet performance achievement standards to create a new reality based on success, not failure.

Today, I have bounced back, thanks to some positive supportive services, motivation and encouragement to "Believe Again." **The UP L.I.F.T. Project**. will be established as a Not-for-Profit 501 (c) 3 organization, and with the assistance of some world renowned psychologists, educators, physicians and counselors, the project curriculum will be able to meet the needs of youth struggling to figure it all out so they can reach their full potential.

I will commit my time and energy to travelling throughout the nation, raising funds to deliver a message of inspiration and hope to our future generations. I am asking you to help me decrease the failure rate of teenagers by increasing their success rate. Help me increase students' test scores by increasing their self-esteem and inspiring them to dare to dream, challenging them to believe in all possibilities, and revitalizing their hope for a better tomorrow. Your support will help positively impact the future of a troubled teen, like I once was. Love, support, correction and inspiration changed my life and I am now committed to a cause larger than myself. Please help me to elevate the lives of young people everywhere. Together let's decrease the dropout rate by increasing the attendance rate. Let's decrease teen violence by stimulating teen respect, love and appreciation for their lives and the life of another. Together we can decrease the suicide rate by sharing the inspiration of joy to impact the success of teens everywhere, I can be reached at 708-673-3439 or email me at juliusmercer6doc@gmail.com

CRISIS IN AMERICA

In March of 2007, I contemplated the youth crisis and conditions in America, and I thought, "How can I make a positive difference? How can my life make an impact?" From there, I began to develop the structure of a powerful motivational live entertainment program geared to alleviate the teenage crisis facing America. It resulted in The UP L.I.F.T. Project, which stands for "Living Inspiration For Teens"...*empowering while creating a new awareness that makes them think about themselves in a whole new way or simply to feel loved or appreciated.*

Hearing about and seeing dismal statistics over the years on the rising dropout rate of elementary and high school students in the United States, and on the low graduation rates of African-American males increased my concern for the plight of American teens of all ethnicities. The alarming number of African-American and Hispanic Males incarcerated due to drug involvement is staggering. Substance abuse and a lifestyle of

1

selling drugs, are the results of a bigger issue. In other-words, these two things are the effect and therefore, it is imperative that we do the best we can to understand the underlying causes. You are about to read a few true stories which will help you to a gain deeper insight and broader understanding of the lives of others who have struggled, and then with some encouragement brought forth "a new fire in themselves."

I know firsthand what it is to suffer in silence while reaping all of the negative benefits that come with the fears created by negative thinking. I lived this "crisis in America," living with fears in the classroom, at home, and throughout society. Fear told me to be quiet and not say anything or ask the teacher any questions because I was afraid other students would make fun of me. Fears like, "I'm not that good at this so I don't want to embarrass myself, so don't even try." Other fears that I really regret were thinking that learning how to use a computer was too hard for me, understanding and succeeding in Biology was not my cup of tea, and being able to achieve good results in Mathematics was something I could not do.

These were fears I was facing in silence; I was an American teenager in a crisis. I had unresolved issues that I decided not to talk about because I believed no one cared enough to listen. Most teenagers in crisis believe they have to go through this struggle on their own because it would be too embarrassing to share with others. Today, 30 years later, I am computer literate, and I've embraced math as a vital ingredient in understanding my personal and business budgets. Biology became my friend as I succeeded in the World Track and Field Arena. I overcame these fears or obstacles in my life by speaking up and asking questions. I learned that there are no stupid questions. I began questioning my instructors, regardless of the outcome.

I began to understand that not only did they sincerely care about me, many teachers, instructors or professors actually care about all of their students. Teachers want each student to reach their highest potential and beyond. I reached out to my instructors and asked them to assist me whenever I would get confused or needed further clarification about something I didn't understand. It was then that the assignments and projects

3

became clearer and the quizzes and tests began to get much easier than I ever thought possible. I began to actually engage the educational learning experience with a sense of optimism, not fear. I made a conscious decision to break this chain of fear and doubt by developing good healthy relationships with people that had a positive attitude and outlook. A former employer of mine; "Thresholds Psychiatrics of Chicago, Illinois Rehabilitation Services," was primarily responsible for my becoming computer-literate. I am honored to have been a former employee of Thresholds, Inc. My co-workers there were very compassionate, intelligent and fun people to work around.

They provided me with the opportunity of a lifetime, even after I made them aware of my bout with depression. They explained to me that the combination of my working there and having practical experiences with depression, substance abuse and homelessness would be a plus to their program and an example that the program really can assist others who are suffering from these issues.

Another employer that aided in my recovery, advancement and knowledge was an agency called Aunt Martha's Youth and Family Services of Park Forest, Illinois. They gave me excellent training and hands on experience working to assist young teens and families dealing with legal or court related issues through the Department of Children and Family Services. There are a couple of individuals I would like to personally acknowledge as very special to my growth and development. Vernola Baskin and Ms. Lannetta Albright are people who genuinely care about their staff and clients. They were my supervisors and have an innate God-given drive to inspire and motivate. I learned a great deal from them and I admire and respect their passion. They were always available to listen to all of my personal and professional concerns. They represent that which is good and pure about effective leadership. They have great listening skills, and in my opinion they were extremely flexible and patient, yet firm when necessary. I believe that these are three of the most important qualities that make up any good human being. It is also my view that the values of confidence, courage

5

and faith are the basic ingredients that allowed me to attain tremendous heights of achievement in track and field. Today, those same values continue to provide me with a solid foundation as I climb this ladder of recovery and success. Today, in my hometown there still exists a "Crisis in America" among the teen community. Our teens are not very far removed from the experiences, struggles and challenges of our neighboring city, Chicago. In 2008 and 2009, Chicago saw an alarming rise in the number of teen related crimes of violence, particularly around the high schools which are considered "safe zones." My purpose and passion for life now extends beyond the boundaries of self- preservation. I am committed to a larger mandate; to reach and teach, to inspire and challenge this generation of teenagers to live life through the experiences of joy not hate, respect not jealousy and ultimately to accept responsibility for making better choices. As I came out of this "Crisis in America" experience, I learned not to dwell on the wreckage of my past or to worry about the future, which can destroy a person, but to instead accept the NEW FIRE in ME!

Out of this "Crisis in America" has come a NEW FIRE! – The
UP L.I.F.T. Project.

THE POWER OF FEAR

What are the most important things to you? Money? Love? Having fun? Partying? Courage? Happiness? Is it Passion, freedom, respect, health, or family? If you are struggling with certain areas of your life, I am asking you to review what you value the most and figure out if these are the values that guide your decisions. Our values can have an important impact on guiding our decisions and life choices.

I spent eight years of my life incarcerated from 1996 through 2007. While in prison, I attempted suicide and was sent to a mental facility three different times. It all began with my divorce, which devastated me, and very soon after that I had to endure the untimely death of my father. He actually died in my arms. Almost immediately I became angry at the world, God, the police, and the paramedics. This anger caused me to suffer a severe depression. I just did not care anymore. My attitude about these events changed my outlook on life.

Before my depression, my values kept me on track and kept me from doing drugs or hanging out with those who violated the law; but the depression weakened my values and began leading me down a path of self-destruction. Soon, I began to spiral downhill at breakneck speed. Not only did I start hanging out with people who used and sold drugs, I began to get sucked into the drug culture with them.

I now had two huge problems, deep depression and a drug addiction. Values are also part of your moral belief system: what you feel is right or wrong. We learn values from our parents and teachers, and as we continue to grow, we mix some of those values with those of our peers and friends. This mixing or changing of values can be either harmful or helpful, depending on who we allow to influence us.

How could this have happened to a person like me? I was an Illinois Track and Field high school state qualifier, participating in the 330 low hurdles, and in 1984 I was ranked number six in the United States, which enabled me to receive a full scholarship to a major university. I was once remembered as a dynamic athlete who competed in the1984 Olympic trials and was inducted into the prestigious Sports Hall of Fame at Kansas State University by an accomplished and caring social worker and substitute teacher. How could such a strong, positive, high energy person like me have risen to such heights, only to fall so far down into the valley? Many times some of the students I had helped saw me on the streets with my dirty clothes on; depressed, hungry, with uncombed hair and sleep in my eyes. Two of my former high school students I helped to believe in themselves sat in the same jail cell as me. While in jail, four of my former mental health clients shared the same tier with me.

Do you know that your beliefs can hold you back from learning or experiencing new things? Belief has the power to create and the power to destroy your capacity to live. Every one of us has a wonderful power deep down inside of our hearts. We all have what it takes to make a difference in this world, for ourselves as well as others. It's a special gift and must be handled carefully and with purpose. But because of our everyday life frustrations, we stop putting forth the necessary positive effort into those things that will make us a better and more productive member of society.

How many people saw the movie "The Pursuit of Happyness"? Will Smith played Chris Gardner, a real life individual who showed up to a job interview. Seated before him was a panel of some very powerful corporate executives at a brokerage firm. Gardner showed up to this interview of his career with paint in his hair, wearing grubby clothes and breath that could knock down a dinosaur. He got the job, not because he smelled bad, but because of his beliefs and values. His values were the threads of beliefs sown deeply in his heart and soul which shaped and molded his character. His values were family, integrity, courage, determination, perseverance, communication skills, self-control, and most importantly; when he was hurt and angry he did not use alcohol, drugs or fall into depression. He simply BELIEVED! When I first watched that movie, I cried like a baby. Afterwards, I called my mother and said through tears, "That's me!" She asked, "why are you crying," and I replied, "I don't know why mother, but I can feel his challenges."

Billionaire Bill Gates came up with some ideas to help millions of people around the world, this is a part of the secret to his success, he BELIEVED!

In order to keep yourself in a higher position or standard to achieve your goals, you have to BELIEVE that you can do it! Have you ever felt like you were not talented enough, smart enough, good looking enough or popular enough? The answer to overcoming these negative feelings and living victoriously is to have a desire to do better. Don't be intimidated by those who would tell you that you can't achieve greatness, because the answers are not in them, they are in you. You have the power within you. The power is your believing that you can do it. You don't have a problem, they do, and their problem is - they have to cut you down in order to feel good about themselves. Unleash your power by making decisions you have been putting off. You won't believe the energy and excitement this will create for your life. That's why I am here today, because I followed my ideas and beliefs to help others achieve success in their lives. I have a passion and I BELIEVE! Just don't quit!

Here are some of the negative beliefs many of us hear while growing up. You're stupid; you are not smart enough to go to college (I was told that); you will never be rich; you can't do anything right; you are not good enough so why should you even try; people aren't interested in what you have to say; boys don't cry; nobody cares what you have to say.

I have learned that if you always do your best, the outcome will be positive. Doing your best is the spirit of constructive passion. When you dive headfirst to beat a baseball throw aimed to get you out at home plate, not worrying about getting hurt; that's passion. It is passion that drives an inventor to keep going until their dreams become a reality. Great ideas help and improve our life conditions.

To stop dwelling on those negative statements, I had to figure out how they ingrained themselves in me, and kept me from learning more about myself and the great things I am capable of achieving. For instance, how do I stop the fear of feeling stupid if I ask a question. My grades in high school were low because of this fear. I was the type of youngster who always wanted to learn new things. When I believed I could do things right, I saw that I got better at doing them; and each time I did those things, I got better.

Once you create a new belief, you need to plant it in your mind by repeating it over and over again as often as you consider your thoughts about yourself. Psychologists say that 90% of our behavior is habit.

There are hundreds of things we do every day by force of habit. We shower, dress, eat breakfast, shop, and clean the house or our room. Some of us get stuck in a rut because negative thinking has become part of our bad habits. We have to change these negative strongholds. We have seen, heard of, or even read about people who have achieved great success in the world. These great individuals became great, I believe, because they found something for which they were willing to go all out. These great people erased fear and found their passion and power. Find your passion, which fuels your heart and soul. Say to yourself, God has put into me everything I need to be successful.

CAUGHT UP WITH THE "WHY'S"

Don't hang around people with bad and negative attitudes. Stay away from those who always cut you down around others in order to inflate their own egos. Run from those who like to fight and argue and are hot-headed. This applies even if you are in a close relationship with someone. If a relationship is constantly argumentative, always remember, you have a destiny to fulfill. Don't get caught-up in someone else's bad habit or outlook.

What happened? This is probably the most common question posed to people who reach high levels of success or celebrity status early in life. For me, it started when I began to focus on the negative things like why and how I was doing wrong. Why me, why do these things happen to me when I have tried to treated others respectfully and fairly? I became really frustrated; why is the world this way when it could be better? You see, whatever you focus on the most is often what you will end up becoming. I chose to focus on the negatives;

16

the bad treatment and unfairness, and as a result, I became a negative person. Little did I know, I was giving up on my future hopes and dreams. Anger directed inward equals depression. While a person can be born with a chemical imbalance or depression, meaning it's endogenous; most depression is caused by over-thinking. What we perceive or feel is a negative emotion that makes us angry is actually a warning sign that something needs our attention. When we become familiar with this sign, then the emotion will become your friend. I lied to everyone I had cared about, telling them that I was all right, except for a couple of my friends, Rich and Sandy Reynoso.

One month after my divorce, my dad and I began to nurture the most meaningful bond I could have hoped for. That bond was built on honesty. Dad recognized that I was at the end of my rope. It was his honesty and transparency, noting examples from his past, that solidified a stronger bond of positive affection, love and openness. This allowed me to express my anger and share my problems positively and without negative rebellion. His openness and honesty provided a sense of relief and let me know that I was rebelling for no reason, which caused conflict in our relationship.

Then suddenly and without warning, my dad died in my arms from a massive heart attack. His very last words echoed endlessly through my mind.

"Help me son."

Neither the paramedics, led by a high school friend of mine, Paul Hodges, or my panicked life-saving attempts could put the breath of life back into my dad. I watched helplessly as the cardiac monitor flat-lined. My mom yelled, "Is everything alright Julius?" Caught up in a whirlwind of anger, disbelief, shock and hopelessness, I couldn't muster enough courage to give a response or to tell my mother and sister that dad had passed away.

I immediately regressed and entered into the world of severe depression. The accumulation of stress from my divorce, the death of my father, and bad memories overwhelmed me and dropped me into a state of manic depression. Sadness and depression are two different things. Sadness comes and goes with a partiuclular situation or circumstance. Depression starts out as sadness, but soon keeps building up; going and going no matter what. I cried a lot and couldn't sleep unless I had a drink. I was constantly thinking about my problems 24-hours a day.

I suffered in silence; disguising the suffering to a certain extent, or as best I could. I seemed to be exhausted, had a loss of appetite, and began to losing interest in almost everything. My self-esteem was at an all-time low.

Bad memories, conscious and sub-conscious, kept me awake during the night. I began making very poor choices including having many sexual one-night stands. Promiscuity began to take its toll and eventually landed me in relationships where hard drugs were commonplace. I underestimated the deadly powerful combination of untreated depression, unresolved issues, hurtful memories, and man-made synthetic drugs. This dangerous combination triggered a neuron-chemical imbalance called psychosis. I'm blessed and cursed to be able to recall the many delusions and hallucinations I had so that I can share it with you in this book.

I was hearing voices and sounds that were not verbalized. I was running from emergency vehicles. Paranoia had me believing they were all a part of an assassination team. The most painful recollection that sometimes brings tears to my eyes was how the psychosis tricked me into believing that my family was part of the plot to kill me and that I would have to take my own life or theirs before they all killed me. I had become spiritually bankrupt. For the very first time, I now truly understand how real post-traumatic, post-partum stress and depression is, along with other facets of pre-disposed mental illness or an illness that is the result of unresolved bitter anger and explosive negative thoughts and how they have impacted our society.

The Honorable Congressman Bobby Rush of Chicago speaks with great concern about this sickness. Throughout the years, there have been news reports of women driving their vehicles into deep waters or people who have thrown children out of windows, reports of terrible child abuse, death, and how this deadly cycle has taken the lives of many innocent people who still had lives full of potential.

While employed in the field of social services, my training certification classes taught me the details and complexities of severe mental illness, however I had no idea that real life practical experience would soon be my teacher.

I had no clue of its actual effects. So please believe me when I say the laws cover the plea of "not guilty by reason of insanity." Untreated depression will become severe, and its severity told me to get a knife and kill myself or my family. Only the grace of God's divine intervention stopped me and told me to put the knife back. I firmly believe this was not an illusion, but a true miracle. My mother and sister never knew this happened. A few hours later, my sister and mother took me to the hospital for treatment. Thank God for their unconditional love and the love of family that would stand beside me and see me through all my nightmares. I began to recall how my dad and mom were raising us as children, teaching us to respect all adults, regardless of their skin color or ethnic origin.

Then everything was confusing and scary, even shocking, as I saw and heard racial bigotry in plain sight. While living in Virginia when I was nine, during the time of school desegregation, I wanted to hide on the school bus from racial riots initiated by the KKK. Dad was a military man and took time off from work and followed the Army National Guard to and from each county until the tension eased.

It was as if my mind was stuck on negative memories and set on instant replay. I couldn't shake the thoughts of how this hatred wouldn't allow blacks to lodge at hotels/motels overnight because we (blacks) weren't welcomed there.

Dad did not like the idea of driving around the Smokey Mountains because there was a winter storm in progress that made it too dangerous to drive through. Dad was so very angry about the bigoted attitudes. We could see it in his face. However, he somehow managed the strength and courage to refrain from exposing his true feelings around us. He bought a

22

loaf of bread, mayonnaise, some bologna, gassed up the car and said, "Let's go." He then skillfully but slowly drove all night non-stop through the Smokey Mountains, intermittently telling us to "hold on if you have to pee."

Then the affliction of racism took another turn as we arrived in Illinois, specifically, in the southern suburbs of Park Forest, Illinois, in 1973. I was now 13 years of age, and my two eldest brothers, Mike and Fred were direct targets of physical and verbal abuse from a secular fascist group of young radical white men who classified themselves as "Nazis." They would spend their days terrorizing people of color or whites who were friends of or even socialized with people of color. There were many weekends and evenings when a close friend of mine named Khallis and I were racially assaulted; hit by hurled bottles, beers cans and sticks while on our way to play basketball and table tennis at an after school program.

The same group that accosted us placed stickers all over the Park Forest community that read "white power" and featured a Nazi logo. In 1976, my eldest brother and his friends were attacked by at least 15 to 20 Nazis at the Park Forest Plaza. My brother Fred was hospitalized, which so angered my dad that he went looking for the Nazi gang with his Excalibur gun. He didn't find them but my Dad spoke with the police chief, who assured him they would apprehend the thugs. Within one week, the police had captured the assailants, dispersed the group, and Park Forest has since become one of the greatest all-American cities in the nation. This was, in large part, due to the city's cultural diversity. Folks of all ethnicities grew up together in a relatively peaceful neighborhood, and there was a low crime rate and few racial confrontations.

Then unexpectedly, the big BOOM! My marriage was ending, under the terms of "irreconcilable differences." It all ended after a seven-year span. Six of these years were the greatest years of our lives. We enjoyed many wonderful, joyous and adventurous times. We had FUN! We were both exercise, health and fitness nuts, and we had lots of fun together. The seventh year brought a whirlwind of decisions, issues and changes. My wife was pregnant with our first child. I was extremely happy but found myself unable to deal with the changes that go along with pregnancy like adjusting to a major reduction in physical intimacy and emotional affection. Perhaps this was an indicator of some immaturity on my part, but regardless, our relationship was changing. A relationship that was once built on mutual compromises, mutual trust and respect had degraded to uncompromising differences and feelings of rejection on both sides. We divorced when our child was two months old. My hopes of reconciliation were destroyed when I learned that my former wife re-married within three months of the divorce. I was caught up in the how and why's. Just five months ago, when my child was born I was elated. I was the happiest man on earth and now I was crushed.

The Lamaze pregnancy training classes were helpful, but they could not prepare me for that moment when our daughter was born and they said she wasn't breathing. I panicked, and screamed, "Oh no!" They said that her esophagus and nostrils were closed with defecation. The doctors quickly attempted to clear the blockage by using a syringe as a siphon technique. I yelled her name, "Jessica!"

She opened her eyes, stared at me and then began to cry. I cried too, realizing that a miracle had been born. I cried so much that I could barely see. I looked forward to showing her off to everyone in my family, everyone I knew and everyone in the entire community of Park Forest.

During the course of my divorce, I voluntarily surrendered my paternal rights to my ex-wife and her new husband due to my illness of depression. It was one of the most painful decisions I had ever made in my entire life, however I thank God that I had the wherewithal to not be so self-centered, but be willing to do what was in the best interest of my child. My Dad advised me to just focus on getting myself together and that someday my biological daughter would search for me, and guess what, she did! I had to learn to stay focused daily, because the temptation to stray lies dormant, awaiting my every move. Spiritual maintenance, especially thankful prayer has become a daily routine.

In retrospect, there were many factors that led to my divorce. Our inability to compromise, my inability to cope with the hormone changes that my ex-wife went through, and my own psychological and emotional changes, along with some self-centeredness on both our parts destroyed what was once a relatively beautiful relationship. My wife and I considered health and intelligence high priorities, and this seemed to lead us through a short successful relationship, but it was ultimately unable to sustain our relationship through the big important changes of life. Obviously, we didn't have the fortitude and passion to overcome the difficulties of life together, or the maturity that comes with adult development.

It was not easy, and the words strong commitment, daily practices, and eliminating weaknesses are what drove me to focus on improving my strengths to become a champion hurdler in world-class track and field competition. In high school, Coach Larry Roland (Rich East High School) motivated me to join the track team after being referred by my eldest brother, Fred. At that time, Rich East had an extremely talented track team;

among the best in the State. In 1979, my hurdling skills were being developed at a tremendous rate, especially considering I was relatively new to the sport. My hurdling buddy and teammate, Donald Hudspeth, signed a letter of intent to Butler Community College in Kansas. You might remember, earlier I mentioned that my failure to embrace the academic learning experiences and place a high priority on making good grades kept me from going to a major university after graduation. However, junior college was still a viable option. Local high school track coaches in the area nick-named me "the Doctor" of the hurdles, and coincidently, the Manhattan, Kansas newspaper columnists who covered Kansas State Sports, wrote articles and used the same nick-name that was given to me when describing my races. When I attended Butler County Community College, I had a unique workout routine; I pulled sleds made with a piece of carpet to fit as a vest while dragging a 150 lb. log up and down hills to gain upper and lower body strength. Coach Francis also had me doing 100 yard sprints repeatedly, along with sprinting quarter-mile turns into 40-50

28

mile per hour headwinds. As a result of such a disciplined and vigorous routine, I earned the honor of being named to the Junior College All-American 1st Team Track and Field 110 and 400 Meter Hurdles. I was the first and only track athlete to accomplish this feat in Butler County's history, a record which stands strong today.

In 1983, I placed first in both the 110 and 400 meter hurdles at the "Big Eight" Conference Championships held at the University of Oklahoma. Then I placed third at the National Collegiate Athletic Association (NCAA) track and field championships in Houston, Texas.

Kansas State Coach Steve Miller enforced a rigorous training regimen that included:

1). No days off
2). 3-mile runs, twice per week
3). 6-mile runs once per week
4). Swimming pool workouts
5). Big Hill workouts

6). Weight-training

7). Watching our diet

I learned that self-discipline and an attitude of commitment to track and field paid huge dividends. These preparations strengthened my abilities, and the verbal repetition of the right priorities gave me the number one variable needed for any successful situation - confidence! I could hear Coach Miller's voice in my head just before I began each race. "You've learned everything you need to know and you're in great condition, so go for it!" I was committed to the mindset that "I can do it!"

THEY'RE JUST LIKE ME

I tend to push harder when things are going well. However, when things weren't going so well, I became hard on myself (have you had this feeling before?). I had to work on improving my attitude; finding the right balance and discovering the positive lessons that come out of bad situations.

Rather than live in accordance with the good values taught by my mom and dad, the values that once held me to a good and healthy set of high standards; I took another route where they were no longer a part of my being. I was living a life of pain and pleasure. As a result, promiscuity had gotten the best of me. As I mentioned earlier, I began to look for quick gratification in terms of affection through prostitution, which ultimately led me down a dark path of drugs, despair and destruction of self-esteem. I had to take several AIDS tests which fortunately proved to be negative. Fortunately, I did not contract any STD's. As bad as it was, I also learned a lot about people with more severe drug habits then me. We all suffered from the very same things, such as depression, a relationship gone sour, death of a close loved one, physical or mental abuse, or rejection and bad memories of unresolved issues. In the midst of my promiscuity, I had a child out of wedlock. I initially rejected her, because the mother told me it was between me and another man. Her family and mine believed the little girl looked just like me. When I saw this beautiful little girl at the age of 2, I saw features similar to mine.

My drug habit had now really spiraled out of control, and consequently, I was only in her life for five months out of her 7 years. This, knowing that I was not a good father also added to my imbalance and lowered my self-esteem. At times I really felt a sense of total helplessness, and all of these experiences were being left untreated.

Destruction was almost imminent. Most people who have a heroin or cocaine habit do not continue to smoke (blow) or shoot-it-up just because they continue to enjoy the high, it's because the withdrawal pains are so severe, causing a physical dependence. This one gentleman explained to me that when he decided to quit, he went cold-turkey; and for the next two days he locked himself in his bedroom and was literally crawling on his hands and knees. He instructed his wife not to open the door, come in or give in to his screams or commands to go and find him some heroin. Heroin affects the entire nervous system and once the system is exposed to a certain level or continuous amount, the brain's pleasure center, which is stimulated by the nervous system, develops a massive craving that the average person cannot fathom or imagine. The withdrawal process totally shuts you down physically; virtually shutting down all movement. Drinking more heavily and using hard drugs gave me a temporary sedation of feeling good, and as each day passed, I wanted relief, to feel that false sensation of good. It was fuel to destroy my dreams.

Pride began to be my leader. I began to believe that I was too smart to allow the drugs and depression to do me in like other people, but I was wrong. I was an empty vessel. Emptiness, loneliness, guilt and resentment were my best friends. The innate intestinal fortitude that once helped catapult me to becoming a world-class hurdler was now a mass inside my body and brain, filled with a loss of hope. I was just like them and they were just like me. Ninety percent of those incarcerated in the jails and prisons all have commonalities related to untreated, unresolved family and relationship issues that went horribly wrong.

One of my cell-mates, let's call him Tony, was a 500 lb. male who lived with an alcoholic mother. On a daily basis, Tony stayed filthy-drunk and was physically and verbally abusive. Tony explained how he watched helplessly as one of his brothers died without warning and how he was unable to ride in the ambulance, because he was too busy arguing with others who were inebriated. Tony was charged with domestic violence. Tony felt that these charges were false and were the result of having to deal with his mother during her alcoholic phases. Tony was arrested while his mom slept it off. I then began to share my story with him, hoping it might empower him with the life changing impact of knowing that "*someone else was just like me.*" I believe that a true and intimate relationship with God matters most and is the beginning of recovery and victory, but as much as Tony needed God, he also needed helpful strategies to cope. Tony smiled, wiped his eyes, and we gave each other a high-five. Even in the midst of my own struggles to get back in the race of life, I never gave up. I would somehow get back up. I kept trying again and again, even though it wasn't easy.

Tony decided to try therapy. Therapy can be administered by different types of supportive services such as teachers, counselors, and/or preachers. Personally, I recommend finding a person with refined skills in this field of study. I enjoy telling my story to others because I have seen how it can help others with similar issues. It helps people similarly afflicted to open up, making them feel comfortable, and most importantly, they began to really understand their experiences and feelings.

Holding everything in and not sharing my feelings gave me a false sense of reality. I began stealing from and manipulating my family and friends. Abandoned buildings and abandoned cars were a great relief for my body which was weakened by the drugs and lack of nutrition. I began to look just like them, thinking I was so different. I now realize this unfortunate part of my journey would help me to see the world in a whole new way. They were just like me, someone who had tasted a normal life of experiences, struggles and challenges, but made some really poor decisions. However, with the memories of my parents' values and my coaches' motivational statements, my survival instincts would kick in and bring me back.

EDUCATION IS THE KEY TO SUCCESS

Often teenagers don't place a high priority on the value of education or place intelligence high on their list of values.

During the successful years of my track and field career, I rubbed elbows with some of the greatest athletes in the world. In one year alone, 1984, I met with, became friends of, and competed on the same national platform with some great Olympians such as Al Joyner, Jackie Joyner Kersey (Women's world record holder of the Heptathlon), Edwin Moses (two-time hurdles Olympic champion), Carl and Carol Lewis (Carl the second person to win four Gold medals, while his sister Carol won a medal in the women's long jump competition), Michael Conley of Chicago (long jump and triple jump medalist and Thomas Jefferson from Cleveland (a sprint medalist), Doug Lyte (pole vault medalist), my teammate at Kansas State University, Greg Foster (silver medalist in the hurdles) of UCLA, and my hometown comrade from Maywood, Illinois. Moutawakil of Morocco, a 5ft. 2in. young-lady from Iowa State University, who ran the 400 meter hurdles (this young-lady was barely taller than the hurdle itself) and was the first ever to win a gold medal for her country, and Sundai Uti (Olympic medalist). There was the innocent Ebunike of Iowa State.

These people represented some of the greatest moments in the history of the Olympics, particularly over the past few decades.

My life was going pretty well as a result of learning how important education was. Eventually in life, education will aid in the development of a person's ability to make intelligent decisions, for the most part. Education put me in this world-class atmosphere. During these years, I didn't live too high and I didn't live too low, but I was happy.

While attending Butler County Community College in Kansas, I had some trouble in academics. My weak areas were basic Math, Algebra, and English. I didn't know how to write a complete sentence or put into written words the proper paragraphs needed to correctly articulate my thoughts and complete a written essay. I was on the verge of losing my athletic scholarship due to poor grades, and because I tried to out-slick the track coach by risking injury to play in a basketball tournament in the local City Leagues. Perhaps playing sports gave me a false sense of pride and security, or feeling that I was better than my peers and could get by without overcoming or confronting my academic issues. This can sometimes be one of the biggest struggles talented athletes experience, when they believe they may not have the aptitude to grasp the basic fundamentals of academic studies.

Through the support and counseling of great people at Butler Community College, I began to understand that wonderful physical attributes can only get you so far in life. You are guaranteed to get older and will eventually reach some physical limitations, however your brain has a greater capacity to continue to receive, study, and calculate information, reason logically, and determine solutions and strategies that can offer you the opportunity to continue to explore, create and achieve.

The faculty at Butler assigned me to special classes that would help me overcome my deficiencies. When Coach Francis

39

discovered that I was playing basketball, he chewed me out and threatened to take away my scholarship. I believe his biggest disappointment was that I had been dishonest with him. However, he had a special love for and sincere dedication to his athletes. Once he read me the riot act, it became real to me. I then understood I had a life changing decision to make. I thought to myself, "not my scholarship!" I don't want to go back home. I said, "Coach, please give me another chance!" Coach did not give me a favorable response immediately. Something inside of me said, "Go talk to another Coach." I went and talked to Coach Kohls. He had an uncanny ability to deal with student relations in a very bold, insightful, and compassionate manner, unlike what I had experienced with any other person who was born and bred in Kansas. He commanded, demanded and expected only one thing, and that was respect. He kept it real, and he shot straight from the hip. After explaining my problem, he had a discussion with Coach Francis and it apparently helped to calm my track coach down quite a bit. A few days later, Coach Francis approached me. He apologized for snapping at me and then calmly explained why it was so dangerous and a huge risk for me to be playing basketball (wow, he obviously saw something special in me, that I did not know at that time). He said I want you to enjoy this college experience and have fun. I know that you like basketball, but just be very careful with your decisions, because if you get hurt, no one will want to continue paying for your education and I want you to graduate without having to pay out of your pocket. Later I learned that Coach Kohls and Coach Francis had grown up together. Additionally, Coach Francis' father is a hall of fame track coach in Division II College Sports. For years he produced very successful student-athletes at Fort Hayes State University. Again the concept of positive values being passed on to the children, Coach Francis' philosophy as a coach, I believe, was in some part impacted by his dad's legacy. As of 2009, Mr. Kohls is head of student recruitment at Butler Community College. If you are considering a college to attend or encouraging your kid to attend, give Mr. Kohls a call for a great opportunity to attend a fine institution of higher learning, great sports and an overall great college experience. I am forever grateful to Butler Community College.

Upon my graduation from Butler Community College in 1981, I attended my first recruiting trip to further my education. I visited with the University of Arkansas in Fayetteville, Arkansas, known by many as the mighty "Razorbacks." I was greeted by one of the greatest triple-jumpers in track and field history, Mr. Mike Conley (today he is Mike Connelly, Sr.). Mike Conley came from Luther South high school in Chicago where he held records in the District and State triple-jump events. He won a Gold Medal in the 1996 Olympic Games, as well as countless World Championship Titles. Mike showed me a vision of what I could have as a result of furthering my education and excelling in athletics.

Mike led me on a two-day tour of the Razorbacks' beautiful multi-million dollar, state-of-the-art facility. Then he shared with me the importance of earning a degree. Mike was actually younger than me (a sophomore – 2nd year student), while I was entering as a junior. He had business sponsors supporting his track and field career such as Purdue Chicken, which was based in Arkansas. The things I admired and most impressed me about Mike Conley was his sincere personality and humility; in addition to his emphasis on education. He explained to me that as a teenager he had no idea, or vision of seeing himself as an extremely talented all-around athlete in basketball and track and field. His emphasis and focus was always on education, gaining knowledge, proper application, followed by graduation. Academic excellence was the key to all of his success in the athletic arena. Today, Mike plays a critical role with the City of Chicago and its bid to host the 2016 World Olympics. He is Executive Director of World Sports Chicago. Mike came from the inner-city communities, facing many of the obstacles of growing-up in a big complicated city. If he did it successfully, then so can you. "Education was the Key". Talk, talk, and talk more with your coaches, teachers and counselors. Find out how to go about putting yourself in a position to achieve beyond your potential.

Because of an individual like Mike Conley, my inspiration, focus and drive was highly stimulated to set higher personal standards to achieve by giving my best to both sports AND education.

Meanwhile, news of my success in track and greater potential had spread across the region. I began receiving attention from a number of Division I Colleges and Universities such as the University of Nebraska, University of Oklahoma, the University of Kansas, University of Miami, Florida A&M and a host of others including many Division II Colleges. Ultimately, I chose Kansas State University, home of the Wildcats. There were a number of reasons that I chose the Wildcats, however the determining factor was that I needed financial assistance and they offered a full-scholarship. My motivation was energized by a multitude of relationships with influential people in my life such as Coach Johnny Meisner, Peter Struck, Mr. Hynk, Larry Roland, Roger Bohnesteil, Dale Freundt, and Steve Fisher (current Coach of San Diego State University). All of these people had a tremendous impact on my life as a teenager while I was attending High School. These people taught me the values of hard work and being a good person. They guided me through high school while helping shape my conduct and taught me to be a good person. This is where I learned what "character" meant. I believe many of the things they taught me helped to save my life. Mr. Lionelle Poole, a high school Hall of Fame Track Coach, formerly of Bloom High School-Chicago Heights, Illinois, was responsible for negotiating a full track and field scholarship for me to attend Butler County Community College. He also gave me the vision to believe I could compete and succeed at the Division I level college sports and obtain an academic degree by successfully completing all of the necessary course requirements.

Education was the key, because it put me in a position to be mentored and developed by Coaches such as Hall of Fame track coach, Steve Miller and others like Ollie Isom, John Cappriotti, Gregg Kraft and John Francis, which catapulted me to a world class hurdler.

There were professors at Kansas State University such as Henry Camp and Marvin Kaiser who advised me to put quality time in at the library. They encouraged me to research information on a particular subject matter related to my class assignments or to ask the Librarians for assistance. One of my professors used a very unique and effective exercise with me. He told me to seek out a mentor who overcame great obstacles in their life, then study their life and learn from them. I chose Mr. Frederick Douglas, a man born into slavery during the 1800s. Illiteracy could not stop his internal drive to rise above racial injustices and educational inequality.

As a child, he tricked his slave counterparts into teaching him how to read. He then escaped from being enslaved because he was able to read the directional signs, and headed north to Massachusetts where slavery was abolished.

Arriving there, he eventually found comfort with new friends, married and began a family. He performed well in school and joined forces with other blacks and whites who had formed an Abolitionist Party.

This winning attitude of Mr. Frederick Douglas eventually manifested itself into the development of an incredibly intelligent man. My mentor, Mr. Douglas, was an educated slave who soon escaped physical slavery in the deep southern territories of America to become an icon in the history of the African-American experience.

Everyone in the world has some type of raw talent or potential that can be nurtured and brought out with the help and guidance of the right influences. It takes a combination of people who care to find out what you can offer to humanity, your family and yourself. I managed to excel athletically and academically. Seeing the vision, establishing a plan and setting goals are paramount on the journey. I had a goal to shoot for in track and field; the Olympics. I wanted to become an honored member of the 1984 United State Olympic Team.

Education teaches you how to observe things and research information. I learned to observe my competition and study the best athletes and their techniques. The target of my research were those who had already made a name for themselves, and were considered by their colleagues, sports-writers and coaches to be the best in the field.

My coaches would say, watch how they stretch and warm-up; they would separate themselves from everyone else in order to gain better focus and concentration. To compete against the greatest 400-meter hurdler in the world was my target, the great Mr. Edwin Moses. Edwin Moses, a graduate of Morehouse College, was in a sense my idol. Mr. Moses was an undefeated Olympic Champion in 1976, and he recited the Olympic oath on behalf of the 1984 Olympic team.

Two months prior to the 1984 Olympic Games was perhaps a snapshot of the greatest moment in the pursuit of my goal. Even today the memory, is as vivid as photographic recall; memories of a split-second during competitions in Indianapolis, Indiana at the United States Track and Field Championships. This meet attracted the largest number of media in the history of U.S. Track and Field, particularly for the 400 meter hurdles. Edwin Moses had entered the event with, I believe, 110 straight victories and one more win would set a new record. This fact also allowed me to set the scene of events leading up to the record setting moment of my life.

Nine men had qualified for the final showdown and wow, I had surprised even myself by not only qualifying for the big showdown, but finishing with a qualifying time second behind Edwin Moses. He was in Lane 4 and I was in 5. The race was being televised on a national network by the Wide-world of Sports (the ESPN of my era). These conditions alone gave me butterflies. I'm on the national stage with some of the world's best athletes and I can't believe all of this is happening so fast. As each runner lined up behind the starting blocks, the television coordinator instructed us to relax due to a television time-out, because a major golf tournament was also in progress. During the time-out, I asked Edwin Moses to sign an autograph of a picture for me and I said, "Please sign it to Richard Reynoso, he's a dear family friend of mine." Edwin smiled while glancing at me with his head titled sideways and said, "Are you trying to use psychology Mercer?"

"No!" I said politely. "You're my idol man, my neighbor who trained with me asked me to get your autograph for him if I ever had the chance to meet you." Edwin exclaimed, "Are you serious Mercer?" I said, "Yeah, for real man." He signed it and then went on to win the race. I placed sixth, and with that finish, it ended the season. There is a lesson I must share with you about my experience in this event. Right before the start of this particular heat, as we approached the starting blocks, I heard my coach give me a familiar tip. He said, "Mercer, don't look back." I actually had the lead at one point in the race, but lost my focus when I looked back. As a result, I had to stutter step due to losing my stride going into the eighth-hurdle. Edwin then shot past me, drafting four other guys along with him. I finished the race ranked sixth in the United States. Today, I often have shared this fundamental aspect of competition with many athletes, because I know it probably made the difference for me in this race. Because I looked back for a split-second, I teach young athletes to respect their opponents, but during a race to stay focused on the finish-line, look straight ahead and

50

always try to give your very best and finish strong. You may not always finish first, but the benchmark is to evaluate your success by doing better than you did before. This is the best sign of growth, development and maturity to be measured by any athlete.

I felt I should have placed much higher, but I lost focus. However, the experience was unforgettable and even though I lost that particular meet, I didn't lose my intelligence because education was, and is the key. In the process of running the event of my life, in a single moment in time, I learned humility and character, while meeting a wonderful legend in sports, Mr. Edwin Moses.

During my years at Kansas State University, I had the pleasure of meeting a variety of very good people who became my friends. I really did have a misconception about the people of Kansas.

My early thoughts were formed by my ignorance and perhaps experience with other white and black southerners. I thought they were just hillbillies, rednecks and slow, country black folks. I found that the vast majority of these people were kind-hearted, caring, and down to earth people who enjoyed life, laughter, agriculture and sports. The State of Kansas and its people have always been good to me. They represent some of the finest citizens in America.

Without the proper education, both yesterday and today, I would likely be making misinformed decisions about people for the rest of my life. Education is the key.

My pursuit of educational achievement allowed me to meet a gentleman named Darryl Anderson, who soon became a great friend. It is as if he were my brother. Darryl played a critical role in my life at a time when I was in desperate need of some positive motivation and vision to believe that I could regain my academic eligibility at Kansas State. I was dismissed by K-State for poor academic performance issues and I lost my full-scholarship. Darryl was one of my roommates and a great sprinter in track. As a runner-sprinter, in my opinion, he had one of the most explosive starts from the starting blocks anyone had ever seen. An injury to his thigh muscle later hampered his career, but he did not stop his drive to excel in the classroom. Darryl encouraged me to spend more of my time in the library and utilize my peers who held study sessions. Although I was a very quiet person in the classroom, I bought into his suggestions and strategy to utilize the vast resources available to me, including my academic advisors. Soon I was reinstated by the University, and from that day forward, my life had changed for the better. Eight years had passed since I had spoken with Darryl, then in 1992, we made contact again. I asked him what was the biggest surprise he experienced in his career. Darryl replied, "You Mercer, the biggest surprise was to see you graduate." Today Coach Darryl Anderson has a Masters Degree and is the Head Coach of Men and Women's Track and Field at Texas Christian University. Darryl also introduced me to a friend of his from his hometown of Cleveland, Ohio. His name was Thomas Jefferson (no, not the former President. I'm not that old). Thomas was a rising track star attending Prairie-View A&M University. Jefferson placed 3rd (Bronze Medal) in the 200-meter dash (Karl Lewis 1st place-

Gold Medal, Kirk Baptist 2nd place-Silver medal) during the 1984 Olympic Games in Los Angeles. You might remember that it was at these Olympic Games where Carl Lewis pursued a goal to establish a new World record by winning four Gold Medals, a feat once only before accomplished by his idol, the great sprinter, Jesse Owens, during the 1936 Olympics in the presence of Hitler, in Berlin. Then there was Al and Jackie Joyner, the brother and sister dynamic duo representing their hometown of East St. Louis, Illinois. Al was my roommate during the Olympic trials in 1984. We lived in dormitories on the campus of the University of Southern California at L.A. We played checkers and had some cool conversations about life in general. Al went on to win the Gold Medal in the triple-jump, while his sister Jackie, placed 2nd (Silver-Medal).

Jackie Joyner was a very courageous athlete. She actually had an injury to her leg and was leading the other world competitors in the Heptathlon. During her final event, the 800 meters, her injuries took their toll and she placed second by just 5 points.

Many of my greatest memories are in collegiate and professional sports. Getting an education was the key that allowed me to work with many good and great athletes. I had the pleasure of coaching and encouraging Harry Butch Reynolds, a great track guy and former world record performer in the 1984 Olympic-Games from Ohio State University. He is a true story of resilience. I witnessed Harry running under 45 seconds in the 400 meter run while in junior college. There was no way he was on steroids, but controversy surrounded him when he broke the world record. His brother Jeffrey, a Kansas State graduate, also ran 46 seconds and under, and he was clean as well. Today they are both civic leaders serving youth in their community of Akron, Ohio.

I was involved in the young life of a 15-year old kid named Tai Streets. Tai Streets is a very gifted athlete who played professional football for the San Francisco Forty-Niners and later the Detroit Lions. I really enjoyed the opportunity to be a part of his coaching, training and mentoring process. He was particularly special, because I made a promise to his mother to help him and his sisters to continue to strive for excellence in academics and sports. I made sure that they attended a series of clinics I sponsored, coordinated and conducted in 1992 called "The Gold Medal Summer Track Clinics." The following fall semester I was a substitute teacher in one of his high school classes. I began to learn more about Tai Streets, a bright, talented young man with great potential and very good work habits and ethics for a young teenager. At this point Tai was a Freshmen in high school, and during my training sessions with him, I began to share with him all the knowledge I had gained. We began to discuss the finer techniques of being a great sprinter and the science of running. I never had to repeat things to Tai because he had the ability to comprehend quickly and put it into action. The results were almost immediate. Tai had a very good friend named Chris Blossom, who was a talented sprinter in his own right. Chris dominated high school level track and field until Tai entered the competitions. They began a good natured battle for bragging rights during practices that made them both more competitive. Tai was a pure diamond in the rough, with the heart of a champion. He did whatever was asked of him, he was a coach's dream athlete. His backbone was nurtured by a strong and resilient mother.

Mrs. Streets was highly motivating and caring toward her children and other young people. She formed an AAU (Amateur Athletics) Track club for youth, which began with her own children participating. I got involved and supported her efforts by training and helping with fundraisers to raise money for her programs. Mrs. Streets is a woman I really admire and respect, because she has experienced so much by way of challenges, struggles and a divorce, but despite everything, she held on to the reins and led her family on the road to achievement and success as best she could. Tai Streets continues to give back to many communities by offering his services in a variety of capacities, especially for the youth of America.

For years I have felt a deep discomfort or disappointment in myself for not wanting to have a closer association with some of the youth I helped along the way, due to my own downfalls. Most of them never knew the details before this book. Hopefully, it will give them greater insight and a better understanding of the Julius Mercer of yesterday and today.

My hope is that it will clear any pre-formed judgments they might have if they crossed my path during my troubled and turbulent years. I hope and pray that someday, we will all cross paths again, and if this occurs, we may be able to forgive and help one another. Education is the Key.

Every great act I have witnessed or experienced has come from people giving of themselves to others, or on behalf of an inspiration. Edwin Moses dedicated his performances in the 1984 Olympic Games to his Dad, and today I am writing my book and beginning my **Up L.I.F.T. Project** in memory of, and dedication to my Dad.

PRIDE COMES BEFORE THE FALL

There are consequences to the decisions we make in life. Decisions we make can affect other people, including our family and even an entire community. I ventured down the road of life, full of PRIDE breaking the rules. This PRIDE caused me to experience a painful fall that affected everyone in my life.

I broke a rule in my residential community that states, "Any person or persons who is charged and convicted of committing a felony is no longer allowed to live in this particular town-home condominium dwelling." Imagine if you will, my family had planted their roots there for over three decades. And now, because of my transgressions against humanity and myself, I needed permission just to visit my own mother, sister and family at a place I once called home, in order to prevent potential trespassing violations. If I were to violate this residency ordinance, the property manager, the village management, and the police department would all have the option to evict my family from the town-home association and/or to have me arrested.

Prior to my distress, over many years I had developed a respectful relationship with the village management and police department. The village of Park Forest had once employed my services as a youth leadership coordinator. In addition, Mr. John Joyce and Chuck Saby, who presently holds executive positions in that department were very instrumental with developing a marketing-public relations campaign that helped launch the first Julius Mercer Gold Medal Summer Track Camp which debuted in 1992. They were a blessing to me and the community. I really enjoyed being in a position to inspire, challenge and assist in developing some of the finest young people through sports-education and building character and life-skills as we circulated throughout the Village of Park Forest. Perhaps the pay was not comparable to my background, experiences and credentials; however, this was the least of my concerns. My focus was to provide a safe, positive environment for the youth in my sphere of influence so they could have an alternative to loitering in the streets and getting into trouble. I worked tirelessly to positively influence the next generation because this is part of my life's passion. We had lots of fun and I thank my dad for the words of wisdom he gave me during my youth and during my development working as a teacher's assistant in special education at Rich East High School in neighboring Richton Park. He said, "Son if any of your colleagues ever ask 'how is it that you are able to reach so many students that many of us gave up on,' just tell them, you're fair, open-minded and honest."

One day a Park Forest Police Officer told me, "Mercer, you make our job easier, because of all the time you've invested with these kids.

Character is developed through action and footwork. During the time when my life was in chaos, I can remember the kindness of *"Park Forest's Finest."* There were several times that the police officers of Park Forest could have arrested me for vagrancy, but instead they stopped me from harming myself and encouraged me to get some help for my issues of confusion, depression and helplessness.

There were a few times in my life where I witnessed some crooked cops whose behavior left a bad taste in my mouth, but I must admit that the officers of the Park Forest Police Department, have left a positive impression on my heart. A few of them are genuine in their efforts to execute their duties fairly and with justice. A respectful thank you to former Police Chief Mayama. Under his leadership and on-his-watch, they gave me every opportunity to get rehabilitated. Of course, there were certain circumstances when they had to do more to calm down a guy who is 6"3 and weighs 225 lbs.

Without hesitation, they put me in cuffs when I became a threat to others and myself. One of the officers said to me, "It's for your own good." At the time, I thought to myself, how could being arrested and thrown into jail be for my own good? Maybe you have experienced something similar and thought the same thing.

It wasn't until I had gone through detox that I became honest with myself. The detox process included forcing the drugs out of my system. I was treated medically for depression and then began to speak openly, honestly and thoroughly about every resentment, difference, negative experience and sorrowful feeling I was having.

I gave the uncut version to the professional therapists and psychiatrists, who listened to me without judgment and understood my anger and confusion. It was then that I really begin to see that I had been rescued, not arrested. Yes, I will admit many people tried to help me, but I didn't want their help, I didn't believe I needed their help, and I actually thought I could beat this on my own. I was wrong! Each time I attempted to help myself was an effort in vain. I sank deeper and deeper. This really baffled me because I was Julius Mercer, this champion athlete, who had overcome adversity and perhaps even greater odds on the track and field gridiron.

As I became more educated about my particular form of depression, I began to recognize it was a false sense of PRIDE

63

bringing me down. Keep in mind that from a book sense, I was an educated and experienced social worker, servicing others who did not have practical and personal experience. I am not saying that to be competent or successful as a professional social worker, you need to go through what I did (*please don't try it, this practice doesn't make perfect; it hurts!*), but my experience took on a whole new meaning and made it real for me. I was then able to see it and accept depression as a treatable illness. Keep in mind, the average human being does not realize the depth of the internal mental and physical struggles. Even expert professionals are constantly discovering new problems associated with deep depression and continue learning how to develop new approaches for the treatment and recovery of patients. I learned that false or negative PRIDE can have you believing that you can just make up your mind and snap out of it. Once you have fallen too deeply, this thought process can be dangerous (an Illusion). An average level of mild depression or stress in our everyday lives can be managed and resolved when we talk with someone about what happened today, yesterday, or what is supposed to go on tomorrow. Another positive strategy is the use of positive ideas or changes that we rationally decide to make. Outlets like riding a bike, exercising, or taking on a new spontaneous adventure like boating, camping or concerts, movies and plays can be a source of new energy and inspiration. Meeting new people and sharing common experiences and ideas can also be refreshing.

Today, this is my daily pursuit. The new and improved Julius Mercer has found his vision and passion for a healthy, productive and wholesome life in harmony with others. I was extremely blessed to regain my health and sanity.

You see, my ability to conduct or handle myself in a reasonable manner had disappeared. Because I had reached a very serious level of manic depression, medical procedures became necessary to help me gain a sense of normalcy. There are a lot of good and decent human beings who experience these things in their lives and never recover. They never regain their sanity and die with the disease. Doctors, lawyers, presidents, blue-collar or white collar workers and professionals in their respective lives may need some sort of assistance to maintain their sanity. No one is exempt from sorrow, tragedy, unexpected sudden death, loneliness, racial discrimination, or any number of other life situations that might send them over the edge. It all goes along with the journey of life. I once told someone in an arrogant, unashamed manner that I would never become homeless, but there I was, full of PRIDE. Depression, Drugs, bad memories and PRIDE had me living in the streets. I was spat on and had raw eggs thrown at me. I was stigmatized and ridiculed.

Please allow me to share an important statistical note. A large majority of homeless people have at least two years of college education or have completed some type of pre-vocational training, and 25% are veterans of the armed forces. When a family or personal crisis hits, some people stray away in silence and this may be okay (just to get some time alone), so long as one can keep everything in perspective. Why is it that some people constantly feel insecure or question if where they are at in their life is wrong or not enough? Why is it that some people are never satisfied with who they are and unhappy with who they see in the mirror? I've learned that PRIDE comes before the FALL!

Because of pride I began using a heavy synthetic drug, which then began to adversely affect what was once good and healthy pride to overblown arrogance and confusion. I thought I could use these substances and be okay. Remember, I was becoming immersed in drugs and uncharacteristic behaviors, and compounding the poor decision making were a bunch of unresolved emotional issues.

Thank God for those Park Forest police officers who refused to give me a free pass. They did not discriminate or use my preferential celebrity status against me, but their duty was to serve and protect me from myself and others. They executed their responsibility to help save my life.

Depression can trick anyone into believing that death is better than life. Someone once found me hanging from a pole by my own noose. Even today, I often wonder who was that ANGEL that pulled me down and called the paramedics. My depression led to three suicide attempts, which, according to the law, is a felony in some cases. Official criminal charges issued by the State's Attorney's office were predicated on my mental health status, after an assessment through exhaustive psychiatric evaluations. I actually had no memory, nor could I recall these suicide attempts, and once I was told about it by the doctors, I was in total denial. Not me, not Julius Mercer. Julius Mercer would never try to take his own life. The doctors then went on to explain that I reacted this way because I was not in my right mind.

They continued to explain how important it was for me to talk about these issues that were bothering me and not hold in the anger. If I would have removed my PRIDE from the beginning, perhaps this would never have happened or become so severe. PRIDE comes before the FALL!

DEPRESSION AND MENTAL ILLNESS

My negative outlook on life took shape soon after my divorce. In a sense, I felt as if we had taken a grandson away from my mother and a son from his father. This dwelling on the negative was the finger that pulled the trigger which exploded into a deep depression. Many of our beliefs will limit our success if they are not put into the proper perspective. My Mother and sister Robin were the first to sense that something was going wrong with me. This type of discernment is probably the greatest gift of the Mercer women. Then my father followed the clues and his "gut-feeling" told him to convince me to enter a hospital for manic depression. I was admitted into the Tinley Park Mental Treatment Center in Tinley Park, Illinois, where I was under close supervision for eight days. The thing that is more of a mystery than anything is when I came to my right mind, thanks to the medical professionals and the appropriate medication, I had no memory of how I had arrived there. My father, in his foresight and wisdom; actually persuaded me to

69

pursue this course of action, even while I was literally in a manic state of mind. On the eighth day, I looked around my surroundings and noticed that others were experiencing some form of a mental illness. I actually thought I had a new job and proceeded to glance out the windows and I recognized the streets. I knew these streets, they were Harlem Ave. and I could see the I-80 interstate highway.

"Oh no!" I thought, how could this be! I proceeded to open the only door in an attempt to speak to the security officer on duty. The guard yelled "sit your crazy (bleep~) down!" I responded, "but officer, I work to assist people like this." The officer once again yelled, "sit your crazy (bleep~) down before I give you a shot." I began to cry profusely in a mass of confusion, wondering how this could have ever happened to me. I began to pray and ask God for forgiveness for any and everything I had ever said to belittle anyone or hurt anyone's feelings. I now realize that something was wrong with me; however, I did not understand what it was. I only believed that seeking pleasurable things would make me feel better. Again, pride would not allow me to face this head on. The false pleasures of the drugs were temporary moments, which only made me feel much worse afterwards.

I became a habitual liar and wore a mask of deception that injured my deepest relationships. I could not stay at home around my family, particularly my parents, whom I love dearly and did not want to expose my weaknesses or failures. I would be careful to be sober around the immediate family. A silent destroyer was creeping into my life, a mentally crippling force. I later learned that even my brothers Fred and Mike joined the family in prayers for me to get better while offering encouragement. Support is the true foundation of a family's love for one another.

Believe me, the real truth is that the majority of human beings had, or will come face to face with some unresolved issues at some point in their life. It is, however, our responsibility to handle it by taking a position of control and changing the paradigm.

Road rage or other irritations that begin small but careen into larger events can be the symptoms that, if left untreated, can have a major impact on society. Now, whenever I notice an internal thought becoming negative or becoming overly critical of others, I have learned to recognize it and almost immediately interrupt the thought pattern by replacing it with a positive spin, or an optimistic viewpoint that is sincere or relevant. Many times I might simply say, "but for the grace of God." Determination and perseverance, when focused in the right direction, are very powerful forces within a person. A gentleman named Winston Churchill might have put it best when he said, *"Don't give up, don't give up, don't ever quit!"* It took me a long time to get it right. Many of my close friends thought I would never get back to my normal self. But as bad as things seemed, and as much I repeated bad habits, I knew in my heart that someday, somehow, I was going to have a major breakthrough. Once the breakthrough happened, I knew I would do something special to assist others.

In 1984, I placed third in the United States Track and Field Championships 400 meter hurdles in Houston, Texas. My track coach, Steve Miller, put a subtle, visually inspiring picture of confidence into my mind that even appeared while I was running the race.

As a college freshmen and sophomore at Butler Community College, I earned the honor of being a four–time All-American by finishing in the top three places of the indoor and outdoor national championship meets. Coach John Francis laid the foundation of strength, speed and endurance through his great training routines. He was able to shift my nervousness or paradigm of thought that was limiting my improvement. As a result, at the end of the final race, I placed 3rd, winning a bronze medal. Not a bad accomplishment for a kid who entered the race with the second best qualifying time. Another wonderful thing occurred, the ASICS Tiger Shoe Manufacturing Company became my sponsor, and the more I believed that I could do better, the more amazing things happened. Amazing things happen when you believe you can do better and you put all your energy into improving. I went on to qualify for the Olympic trials and was selected as an outside chance to make the team. I placed 6th at the United States Track and Field Championships in Indianapolis, Indiana. I entered the meet qualifying at #2, behind two-time Olympic Gold Medalist Edwin Moses.

Being chosen to compete on the U.S. International traveling team was a huge honor for me. I traveled and competed in Japan and Edmonton, Canada. I had the honor of meeting Prince Charles and Lady Diana, our hosts in Canada. There were at least 10 other states I had the opportunity to visit while competing. My former Coach, Mr. Miller, was an expert at not allowing negative thinking to take over your state of mind. I was twenty-three years old when Coach Miller said to me, "Life is full of moments."

Determination seems to be a common theme; a central key for people who become healthy, wealthy and wise. They focus on solutions. What are you waiting for? Start thinking of new ideas, be creative, set goals and say to yourself, "I'm going to try new things and experience new adventures." Some of the best decisions I ever made in life came after I consulted with my coaches. If you are a student athlete, I recommend that you constantly talk to your coach concerning problems and career planning. Many times they have already traveled the road you are now on.

I recall a conversation with my former high school track and field coach shortly after my college graduation. I wanted to know why he did not encourage me to attend college or further my education, even though I'd won so many trophies and ribbons while competing for his teams. At one point I was ranked in the top five of Illinois State High School Hurdlers. His answer was, "I'm sorry Julius, I didn't think that you could handle the college level classes." I was hurt and felt insulted. This is why many of us gifted black people never amount to anything. Although I was bitter from not being encouraged to attend college, I still have respect for the opportunities and position that my coach gave me. What bothered me the most was that I came from a string of Mercer brothers: Mike, Fred and Chris. Upon Dad's retirement from 23 years in the Army, our family moved to Park Forest from Newport News, Virginia in 1973. During this time, you could count the number of black people in Park Forest on two hands. We fought through unwanted racial slurs and confrontations, especially my brothers Fred and Mike. Things had gotten so bad for them that the constant anger distracted them from discovering their true potential. Dad encouraged them to join the Army, so they dropped out of school and enlisted in the armed forces. Fred and Mike set high school track records in both running and jumping events. While serving in the Army during the 80s, Fred became an outstanding 400-meter hurdler with a personal best time two tenths faster than my best when I was world class status. Mike was one of the best sprinters and could run 200 meters in 20.88 10.35 seconds and sprint 100 meters barefooted. Imagine if Fred and Mike had the advanced technical access and coaching I had. My brother Chris participated on a state qualifying relay team. The Mercers, Davis and Hicks (Mom's maiden name) have produced many great athletes from

Tennessee and Texas. I am proud to be an alumnus of Rich East High School in Park Forest. It was a good school. The teachers are dedicated and the support from the community had a positive impact on my life.

There were so many others within our family legacy with tremendous successes such as Randle and Brandon Mercer, who were exceptional high school and college football athletes. My cousin Earnest Davis was a professional baseball player and was drafted by the Baltimore Orioles as a pitcher with a 90+ mile per hour fastball. Ray Mercer was a 1996 Olympic Goals medal boxer. Ron Mercer played professional basketball, including time with the Chicago Bulls and several other NBA teams. Candice and Janice Mercer were star track athletes at Evanston Township High School. My cousin, Johnny Lee Jackson, was inducted in the Mineral Wells High School Hall of Fame in 2009. Johnny was a three-star athlete, averaging double figures in basketball. He long jumped 22.9 meters and he ran a 21.7 second 200-meter dash. Johnny Lee was an All-American wide receiver at Ranger Jr. College and an All Lonestar Conference wide receiver at San Angelo State University. He played on the NAIA Championship Team, and shortly thereafter as a professional athlete, he played wide receiver in the CFL on a great team lead by Hall of Fame quarterback, Warren Moon. He then played for the Edmonton Eskimos in the Canadian Football League.

Around the year 2000, my former high school was recognized by the Chicago Sun-Times. The paper featured my high school for its famous alumni and most memorable athletic events throughout its history. All of my friends were mentioned but not me. Resentment was tearing me apart. In my mind, it was as if I was holding words hostage in my head, and those words would turn to feelings, which usually made me very angry whenever I started to think about them. The resentment is always a thought about a person, a situation or a circumstance that occurred, but I did not like. Thank goodness I have had really good therapists who worked with me on not letting this negative thinking get the best of me.

Two of the best therapists I have had are Al and Brek. Both are employed by Circle Family Services of Chicago. Therapy has taught me to let go of resentment. The key is to forgive yourself and others. This can be extremely difficult to do. If you are like me, you want to have revenge on those who have hurt you. How do I forgive myself? By searching out the things I did that I know I shouldn't have done to myself or others, I then focus on the things I did that could have, or did cause harm to others. Then I say in a prayer that I am sorry for what I have done. Even if you are not spiritual or do not believe in God, just say, "I forgive myself and I forgive others," and then go forward with your life. Be happy with yourself, because it takes a very brave person to admit to themselves or to others that they are wrong. This will bring you freedom and peace; filling you with an unbelievable feeling.

Afterwards, I just tell myself to try and not to do this again. Don't fool yourself into thinking that things are not going to happen again because they are, and you just have to apply this method all over again, and it is okay to do so. Then go and do something good for someone. Lend a helping hand to someone in need. You now have redeemed yourself emotionally. You have taken charge and helped to change your emotions and feelings from bad to good. In life, everyone makes mistakes, and we all have done things we are not proud of and really regret. People don't talk about these things for fear of being condemned or judged. Everything is not for everyone, and this is why it is best to discuss most negative feelings with a therapist or release the resentment in prayer. Either way, get rid of the shame! Forgive other people as well, don't hold on to bad feelings because the sooner you let them go and let bygones be just that, the better you will become and the better you will feel, emotionally and physically. You will become a much more focused learner, student athlete, and person. Learning to forgive will stop anger and other negative emotions from building up inside of you. Holding on to resentment will keep you angry and keep your emotions off balance.

I smile today with pride, knowing that as of 2009, I still hold records in track and field at Kansas State University and Rich

East High School high school. I hold the number one spot, a record for the men's 300 low hurdles at Rich East high school and the men's 400-meter hurdles at Kansas State University, as well as the third fastest time in the men's 110-meter hurdles at K-State.

PROBLEMS

Poor decision making and negative thinking during a crisis are normal responses for most people, but don't be afraid to call or ask someone for help or advice. Tell them, "I'm confused" or "I'm afraid," but the main thing is to let them know what is happening with you. A suggestion from someone else just might save your life. When the unexpected divorce and death occurred in my life, I immediately began feeling sorry for myself, which caused a complete emotional reversal. When you hurt and display your feelings through angry outbursts or take on an "I don't care anymore" attitude, begin to drink alcohol excessively or use hard drugs, or begin to get involved with others who commit acts that are against the law; you also hurt the people who care about you the most. Suicide attempts doesn't mean you are weak; it means you are hurting. The desire to end your life can happen to people who keep angry, negative feelings bottled up inside of them, or those unable to shake life's everyday frustrations. These feelings can explode under a variety of circumstances such as experiencing a divorce, death, accident, relationship or other issues that result in a feeling of being overwhelmed, just to name a few. When I am feeling overwhelmed, I have a series of steps that I take. First, I stop what I'm doing and remain still so I can think. Then, I make it a point to only do the most important things to the exclusion of all else. I have found that once I have completed one or two important things, my brain begins to register order. This allows me to continue slowing myself down by telling myself that I'm not a machine, I'm human. Then I begin to realize that I'm back in control.

Our self-esteem is how we feel about ourselves, therefore, we must take actions to regain our forward progress of self-motivation. It takes practice to stop thinking negatively.

Another thing that bothered me for years was how my mental illness negatively affected my decision-making process. This illness had me continuously putting myself in precarious positions. I would have never dreamed of being in situations like warming-up in an abandoned building, sleeping overnight on the floor, riding the Chicago trains until the early morning, sleeping in wrecked cars that were towed to automotive shops, befriending people just so I could snatch money from their hands and run. These inappropriate behaviors became extremely common occurrences. Substance abusers and alcoholics have other commonalities such as domestic violence, blackouts, being argumentative, living in the streets, lacking the ability to control impulses, belittling or tearing down the self-esteem of others and self, and needing to constantly have a drink to settle the shaking hands.

If we would take the time to think about all the good or positive that can happen, even if the good seems a little farfetched, we could make the needed changes. Then we could regain the process of taking a major step to change our direction in order to avoid the pitfalls. If I had to pick one thing that ultimately put me on a stronger and more committed path to change, it would be that I wasn't happy with the way my life was going. In other words, my belief and the ways I envisioned myself living was in conflict with my reality. Yes, there was some pressure from my family and friends, but the biggest pressure was self-inflicted, due to my not living up to my own standards. In order to change, I had to learn to link whatever was slowing me down to pain. I had to make some changes with my belief system.

I now turn negative situations such as a misunderstanding or when I feel I am being disrespected into a self-motivating game. I redirect the internal conflict or anxiety I feel from a negative situation into a goal-oriented experience that I use to motivate myself. This allows me the opportunity to utilize self-motivation and drive in order to help myself. However, the attitude must be focused on change for the better. Once I learned this, I began to set goals and reprioritize my values, which enabled me to make a commitment to study a couple of self-help books an inmate gave me.

I attended Therapeutic Cognitive support group three times a week for 12 months, vowing to humble myself and treat others that were less fortunate than me with respect and unconditional love. My bad attitude, anger, and inability to forgive others and myself, allowed negative spiritual forces to dominate and have power over me. When I gave up my power to make the right choices for my mental health and well-being, I basically gave the reins to the negative spiritual power in my life.

It is my belief that if you treat yourself or others badly then that negativity will come back to you in some way or another. This is called Karma. Yes, I treated my family, friends and people who attempted to help me badly, but nothing can compare to the way I treated myself. I was put out of half-way homes and slept in abandoned buildings, not realizing that I was sleeping on other people's defecation and urine. Huge rats roamed throughout the night, looking for food, I couldn't sleep due to their rumbling sounds. I walked miles and miles, hustling up money to keep my high going. Leg cramps and blisters had me resting on strangers' porches, in hallways, and many times on park benches. I fell asleep overnight in parks and when I woke up, birds would run and I'm sure chirped, "that dead man woke-up." Once I was so thirsty I mistakenly drank urine from a pop bottle someone had tossed in an abandoned building.

Twice I slept in cardboard boxes, once in my dress clothes and a necktie and the other time in an abandoned building. I was cold, lonely, scared, hungry and depressed. All addictions have something in common: a compulsion to repeat the behavior that starts after the first series of drinks and hits, or the first chips in a bag, ice cream, cake, or that first roll of the dice. Whatever it is, you just can't seem to stop.

I have overcome problems and obstacles and been able to achieve and accomplish things because I found joy or something positive to focus on. My pain level had finally reached such an intensity that my brain said, "No more! Enough of this unhealthy living, I'm tired of feeling this way."

Now, every day, to get the same positive response from my brain and get the same natural feelings of pleasure or relief I remember having, not those found in substances, I began to use laughter, jogging, weight lifting, as well as other physical activity and recreational sports as an outlet. Sometimes a good old conversation with a positive twist works as well. I once believed I was too strong to be broken by hard drugs. I now know how terribly wrong I was.

I discovered that helping others gave me a tremendous feeling, but the real question was, "How could I begin to help others when my personal issues are still hounding me?"

I met the most inspirational man when I was incarcerated. He was in his late thirties and sentenced to forty years for a string of armed robberies. He was initially sentenced to life in prison without the possibility of parole. We both attended weekly group support meetings that focused on cognitive changes. At one point he was filled with so much guilt and confusion that he ended up being hospitalized for suicidal tendencies.

However, when he was released from the hospital and sent back to the general population and our group sessions, an amazing thing began to happen. He shared with the group how he believed the Spirit of God wouldn't allow him to follow through with killing himself. His testimony reached the hearts of everyone in attendance. It even had me crying. These were tears of relief, knowing that everything was going to be all right. He inspired all of us saying, "Just because we have an X on our backs, doesn't mean that we are X'd out of everything." I thought to myself, "this is a good brother." He was trying to fight off issues all by himself, just like me. We both never planned to achieve and do great things and then turn around and become a monster to society. We both know we were out of control and destroying other lives, including our own families. We were hurting badly and didn't know how to handle it. Yes, I was taught to "man-up" and handle situations like a man; dry up those tears and get busy. If I had been able to stop the monster early, I would have had a fighting chance to avoid all of this, but by now the monster had become full blown due to my inability to be honest with myself and reach out to grab the waving hands of those who tried to help me. If I didn't make cognitive changes, then my family and children would continue to be hurt by my actions.

How do I get these problems out of my Head? How do I change these feelings from bad to good? A technique I learned to use is by a "Peak Performance." The motivational author, Anthony Robbins, teaches people how to formulate questions that will empower an individual to think differently. He encourages all his readers to share his materials with others, so I do.

One of his exercises is this: I want you to think of a problem that bothers you right this moment. For example, something that bothered me for years was why my dad never attended any of my high school sporting events. The most hurtful memory was when my high school held "parent's night" honors for each athletes' parents. Every one of my basketball teammates' parents showed up, but not my dad. Dad told me earlier in the day, "we'll see son." I explained to him that mom wanted to go. When Dad didn't show and Mom did, I became angry and held on to the resentment. What I learned is that I had a control problem. If other people did not act like I wanted them to or if they did not follow my rules, even when it related to affection and its reciprocity, I would become angry. Therapeutic support classes at Circle Family Services of

Chicago has well-educated psychiatric professionals who helped me understand my control issues, including the harmful effects and emotional impact it was wreaking on me and my loved ones.

The fact is that we cannot change, nor should we try to control anyone's response to anything. However, we can take control of how we respond to a given situation. We can hope, pray, encourage or suggest, but trying to control another's decisions can destroy the natural innate spirit called love. So I asked myself, "Why do you want to have control?" I then realized it was so I could dictate my feelings of pain or pleasure that came from the outcome of people doing what I wanted them to do.

Now you can see how important our values are. They are the real compass to provide direction in our lives. So take some time and think about this one. Is your life being controlled by feelings generated by others? Is your life being controlled by the pursuit of what's most important to you in your life? What can I do about this situation right now? This question allowed me to apply reasoning. This is not by any stretch of the imagination an easy thing to do. However, with practice it can help prepare you to handle situations more rationally then just acting on impulse. I used hypothetical role-playing to assist me. I would make up a situation, and reflect on my past reaction to this crisis. I would then think through the appropriate action and store it in my memory. Also, a big part of my reasoning was evaluating my reaction to other peoples' crisis. I would use empathy, openness, honesty, listening and support to help stabilize them. However, I could not support myself when a major crisis, like a family member dying in my arms, hit me.

In some cases, the only thing you may be able to do in a mental or medical crisis is provide a hug, hold a hand, and let them know you are there if they need to talk, get a cold wet towel and apply pressure to the wounded area until help arrives, dial 911, or just hope and pray. Abusing Alcohol or the misuse of drugs during a crisis is not the answer. Believe me when I say this, because after my buzz wore off, the problems were still there. For some strange reason there are still times when the thought to use drugs runs through my mind. Therapists have helped me by explaining that since I sought pleasure through a combination of drugs and sex, I may subconsciously continue to have these thoughts for several months or possibly years. I have spoken with other men who quit using hard drugs or have abstained from alcohol for several years and they've said at times, they had thoughts as well as dreams about smoking a cigarette even after 20 years of abstinence.

A child has to be guided through their youth and teen years. Therefore, we can conclude that if a child's parents or guardians are teaching and role modeling without positive, upstanding values, then it is likely that the child will have problems relating positively to society.

I believe that many of us don't have a drinking problem, drug problem, or a weight problem; instead we have a values problem. These behaviors can happen because of anger and frustration. The root cause is a symptom of value-related problems of what is most important to you. Again, I asked myself a positive question that helped take me out of my depression. Now, I want you to think of a problem right this moment that's bothering you or any potential problem you see with someone you care about. It could be financial, a relationship problem with a girlfriend or boyfriend, school, work, or with the law.

The questions you ask must have a positive spin to them. Ask questions that will uplift your spirits. For example, What's really great in my life right now? What can I do to make it better? If I change the bad way that I am feeling, what will happen to me? If I party more than concentrate on my school work what will happen? If I concentrate on my health as opposed to everyone else's problems, how will this help me? What do I like about this guy or girl? What is it that I don't like? If you see a person happy most of the time, ask them what makes them so energetic and positive. If you are feeling depressed, it's because you have forgotten all of the things that made you feel good about yourself; the things that made you happy and make you smile and laugh. Right now I want you to think of the funniest things you have seen or heard, or experienced. Was it at the circus, at home, while driving in a car, at a night-club, at school and how does it make you feel?

Questions help us regain direction and consciousness by making us focus on other methods, angles and questions that allow us to see the most important aspects of an issue whenever we're frustrated or confused. That is "TO THINK." When I want to laugh to keep from crying, I may lift up my arm and kick my legs from side to side, while singing we represent the lollipop kids.

Julius Mercer shoots 2 points
for Rich East High School, Park
Forest, Illinois (1979)

Julius Mercer at 12
months, Bow-legs

Julius Mercer and siblings' (L-to R), Fred Mercer, Julius Mercer, Michael Mercer

(Center) Julius Mercer, among siblings and friends

Julius Mercer, celebrates a double
victory in the 110 Meter Hurdles and
the 400 Meter Hurdles BIG Eight
Conference Championships (1983)
Stillwater, Oklahoma

Chris Mercer (yellow shorts),
anchors the Rich East H.S. (Rockets)
to a seventh place finish, Illinois H.S.
State Track and Field Finals,
Charleston, Illinois (1982)

(From L-to-R) Lorenzo Brown,
Angelo Booker (U.S. International
Track Team, visiting Mizuno
Corp., Tokyo, Japan (1983)

(From L-to-R) Julius Mercer, Coach
John Francis (Butler Community
College, El Dorado, Kansas) and son
Travis.

Park Forest Village President, Patrick Kelley, salutes Craig Hodges, 1992 NBA Chicago Bulls Champions and local Rich East H.S. graduate honoring Craig as the Grand Marshal of the Fourth of July Parade (1992)

Julius Mercer Dunks at the Craig Hodges charity Basketball
Challenge at the Park Forest Plaza, Park Forest, Illinois (1992)

Track & Field News: Archive: Results

1963		
F: 400 meters; S/F: 9/8; D: 19 JUN		
1.	Edwin Moses	47.84
2.	David Lee	49.50
3.	Andre Phillips	50.02
4.	James King	50.09
5.	Mark Patrick	50.22
6.	Julius Mercer	50.31

Julius Mercer, practicing hurdling routine at Bloom High School, Chicago Heights, Illinois, preparing for 1984 Olympic Trails

A night out with Mizuno Corporate Representatives at Tokyo, Japan (1983)

(From L to R) friends of Julius Mercer, **Mike Jennings**-CEO ON U signature collection, **Anthony "Tony" Mealing**-Dir. Of Physical Ed. / Sports Administrator of Aspira-Haugan middle school joined by Jamal Malcolm Warner (*Acclaimed T.V. & Movie Actor*) and Dwayne Wade Sr. (*Founder of Pro-Pops Foundation and Dad of NBA Player Superstar-D. Wade*) Photo taken at an event sponsored by "Athlete's Against Drugs." (Summer 2008)

Senior track photo at Kansas State
"Wildcats" Julius Mercer (1983)

On The Mark

By Mark Janssen

It's refreshing

In today's world of athletics it seems that the big bucks and egos have taken over.

For this reason, a series of quotes coming out of this past weekend by Kansas Staters or former K-Staters were most refreshing.

Only a handful of days after being in Manhattan for the ninth annual Jim Colbert Celebrity Golf Tournament, Colbert won the Colonial National Golf Tournament in a six-hole sudden death playoff.

The television microphones were able to catch the first words from Colbert to Fuzzy Zoeller, the man he had just defeated for the $72,000 first prize.

Colbert's response was, "You could have had the money...I wanted the championship."

Here's a golfer who after 18 years in the pro golfing business still relished the sense of victory more than the dollars and cents of the game.

Other words helping to restore faith in today's athlete came from Julius Mercer of the Kansas State track team.

Mercer has turned himself into one of the premier hurdlers in the United States and only this year has tasted the satisfaction of victory on the big time level.

Following two gold medal performances at Saturday's Big Eight Championships, Mercer offered this after his second win: "I'm just happy to contribute the points to the team total. We want to win (the team title), but would be happy with a second or a third. I just hope these points can get us in the top three."

Mercer had just completed a rare Big 8 double win in the high and intermediate hurdles. What Mercer talked about was not individual performance, but helping the Kansas State team.

The third quote came from former Wildcat basketball great Rolando Blackman, who was asked about the player who impressed him the most in the National Basketball Association.

His answer was Philadelphia 76er's everything Julius Erving. But it wasn't because of his big scoring average, or number of rebounds, or his glide through the air scoffers.

What Blackman said about Erving was this: "He's just fantastic. The way he conducts himself, the way he speaks and communicates with everyone, his sportsmanship on the court. He's a great example for everyone in the league."

What Blackman saw in Erving is an outstanding compliment to the 76er's No. 6. But at the same time, it says a lot about Blackman for being able to see those qualities in another individual.

Just as it says something about Mercer who was thinking of his team instead of his own accomplishments. Just as it identifies the type of person Colbert is to say the buck with the money, it's the satisfaction of victory that's good enough for me.

Three Kansas Staters that all of us can be mighty proud of. Jim Colbert, Julius Mercer and Rolando Blackman.

Manhattan Mercury Newspaper Article features an excerpt about Julius Mercer titled, "It's Refreshing"

109

Julius Mercer (Center) with high school track and field teammates, Rich East High School, Park Forest, Illinois (1979)

Representing Rich East will be (front, from left) Tom Hires and Dave Paxton. (Back row) K. C. Keeney, Julius Mercer and Brian McMahon.

CRAIG HODGES

CRAIG HODGES, CURRENTLY THE SHOOTING COACH FOR THE
LA LAKERS, THE THREE TIME NBA 3-POINT CHAMPION

Craig Hodges
3-Times NBA (Professional Basketball Player) 3-Point Champion at NBA All-star game (1992)

Carl Lewis, *4-Time Olympic Gold Medalist 1984,* Olympic, Los Angeles, California

Silver medalist Jackie Joyner competing in the heptathlon events.

Silver Medalist, Jackie Joyner competing in the heptathlon events 1984 Olympics, Los Angeles, CA.

113

Edwin Moses his 105th Consecutive Victory
in the 400-meter hurdles, 1984 Olympics

Julius mercer of Kansas State University shows his form, while competing at an Indoor Track meet (1983)

Julius Mercer competes at the 1981 NJCAA
(*National Junior College Athletic Association*) Track and Field
Championships, 3rd Place Finish

CHANGE IS GOOD

I have grown to learn and accept gays and lesbians as people, and although I may have an opposing view of their preference, I have respectfully learned not to judge them. During the time I was incarcerated I noticed there were a lot of gay men in the prison system, and they had no shame about it. They didn't hide their identity and they didn't care what others thought of them. I would see fighting among gay men and straight men. Straight men would, at times, act as if they didn't know the gays when they were in my presence. Some gay men even tried to hit on me, just to see if I would "holla" (communicate or exchange conversation) back at them, but it just wasn't my cup of tea. Prison is no place for anyone. There were many sleepless nights filled with the sounds of sexual abuse. I entered a deep depression from feeling and experiencing a loss of freedom. I learned to carry myself in a certain way to avoid being sexually assaulted in prison by the gangs. When approached, I would become fighting mad, and start using profane language while threatening them. I had at least three fights and a handful of confrontations with gang members, all because I wasn't a member.

I did not fight too much growing up. In fact, the last fight I recall was at the age of 12. And here I am now, fighting for my life at 36, 40, and 43 years of age. When I initially arrived at prison, I weighed 185 lbs. While there, I committed myself to a rigorous regimen of weightlifting, running and jumping rope. Within months I swelled up to 225 natural lbs. of muscle and defended myself from physical pressure and intimidation of others. As a result, several gang members made failed attempts to get me to join their groups. They all began to call me "Red-dogg" a nickname given to me by the "Latin Folk – gang members." Everywhere I went they called me "Red-dogg." I took on the name and demeanor, and that's how I survived in a pit filled with animalistic behavior. I exhibited animal-like behavior when the circumstances called for it. Some gang members who want to change won't do it, because of the pressure to be an active member.

It's important for me today to make intelligence a higher priority on my list of values. Poor decisions have put me in situations that have caused me to adapt and adjust by mixing other people's negative values with mine. I conformed to the peer pressure and allowed it to change me into an insecure, isolated, and distrustful, always-on-the-edge type of man. If this could happen to me in such a short period of time, then imagine the affect it has on 90% of those incarcerated, who began experiencing these pressures from infancy through adulthood. Incarceration doesn't correct the individual; treatment, ongoing therapy and a total psychiatric overhaul may be needed. There are approximately 30 prisons in the State of Illinois and less than half of them have a substance abuse program. There are those who deserve to be locked up and put away. I deserved every consequence that I had coming, however, having access to rehabilitative programs, even after repeating the offenses, was the key to helping me break the cycle.

Eli, a prisoner, serves as a constant example to me. Eli's bad decisions led him to a maximum security prison, where he shared a cell with his son and this deeply troubled his heart, mind and soul. He stayed confused and depressed for several years, but because he never sought a continuous support system of help, he suffered silently and remained in a depressed mode that he just couldn't shake. This mode kept him from overcoming a lifestyle that had him constantly handcuffed and a prisoner of his own mind.

When I was a kid, a famous comedian named Bill Cosby created a cartoon show called, "Fat Albert and The Cosby Kids." The main character was Fat Albert an overweight African-American man with large protruding lips. There was another African-American male character with extra-large protruding lips that would bump together when he spoke. His name was Mush-mouth and his pronunciation of letters and words would echo double sounds. Everyone would laugh at him. I came from a family of African-American males with large lips. After the very first Saturday morning episode back in 1972, many kids teased me by calling me the Cosby Kid. It hurt my feelings so much because it was my own African-American brothers and sisters making fun of me. I took more abuse from them than perhaps any other race of people. I became angry and often cried. For years I wasn't happy with the way I looked, but all of that changed on the day when I was a teenager and this African-American teacher told me to be proud because my lips identified with my African heritage and ancestry.

Did you know that 90% of inmates in prison grew up without a mom or dad due to death or the mom or dad being incarcerated? Many of their parents were substance abusers who suffered from a mental illness. I would say that 80% of those I met in jail or prison had no high school diploma and had difficulty reading and writing. The recidivism rate for repeat offenders is close to 80%.

After the Emancipation Proclamation was put in place, many former slaves were given a few clothing items and enough food for a few days. But they were uneducated, illiterate and unskilled people who were at the mercy of local farmers and sharecroppers. Many farmers had discovered a market for cheap labor, paying very little wages and in some cases they would only provide clothing and housing.

The prison system of today is not that much different. I traveled to four different prisons. The pay was $15 a month for a job which was normally a $10 an hour job and $40 - $60 dollar per month for a $1,200 monthly income job in regular society. The majority of the products produced by prisoners include poultry and bakery items which are sold at markets throughout the country.

Some inmates use their money to pay for protection to keep from being sexually abused. I never had that problem, because when I first went to prison, a correctional officer who worked at a local courthouse instructed me to abide by three rules. "1). Be careful who you talk to 2). Be careful what you say 3). Don't mess with the "sissies." Those were his exact words and I followed them each and every day I was in prison. I heard many sounds of sexual escapades and abuses, and I was sometimes surprised to see many men I thought were straight who were actually gay, having relationships with other men. I was surprised because they didn't act that way around me.

Fighting is very common in jails and prisons. Many people have been stabbed and killed with a shank (knife). Shanks are metal or steel pieces that have been shaved to make a pointed sharp edge. I've seen many prisoners get what is called "pumpkin heads" by being repeatedly beaten on their heads with a sock filled with canned goods. These individuals were hit so often that it caused swelling of the brain. The swelling is so acute that the person's head looks like a pumpkin. I had a lot of lessons to learn in order to survive as peacefully as possible. The most important thing was to try and not resolve a confrontation or problem by fighting someone who belongs to a gang, even if they were the instigators. I had three physical fights while in prison. I was challenged because my demeanor was that of an easy-going, nice guy, non-gang member, non-member of anything.

A non-member was called a neutron, meaning neutral, with no affiliations to any mob organization. I never had problems with the gang members 35 and older. It was mostly those who were 18-30 that seemed to have a chip on their shoulders. They were opportunists. always seeking out whom they could devour. Usually they tried to be slick, be it a card game of trickery, or taxing a person for not paying back money they borrowed. I never claimed to be a fighter, however during my time there I was challenged by those individuals. "Smoking Joe Frazier" came out of me and I didn't have any problems thereafter. In fact, some members made attempts to recruit me afterwards. I grew pretty close to the elder mob leaders because of my athleticism in all the prison activities including baseball, softball, track, ping-pong, volleyball and basketball.

Prison inmates are really big on sports and very competitive. When they found out I was a former world-class athlete, the gang's shot callers (big boss) would put out a protective tent over me to ensure that other members wouldn't start any trouble with me. They also explained to me that if any member gave me any trouble I should notify their superiors, and as long as I did this, I would avoid gang hits. The instigators would receive a violation.

I had to deal with peer pressure. Both negative and positive peer pressure had affected me and my happiness. I lived most of my life being controlled by others, and when I tried to control others, it really meant that I had no control over myself. During one of my counseling sessions while moving toward recovery, I was told that I was somewhat controlling. How did I become this way? One of the training aspects in the field of social service is the theory that behaviors are learned and many males and females suffer from central issues. For me, learning how to be controlling came from my father. During my teen years, dad wanted his ways of thinking to run parallel with mine and my brothers, or he would become angry.

So far, you have read countless behavioral issues I learned or experienced as a child, and not once did I mention drugs or alcohol to be part of the problem. Substance abuse and depression were the end results. My main problem was obsessive compulsive disorder, along with entertaining negative thoughts which were triggered by my dad's habits of always wanting his way.

The fourth and final time I was incarcerated was different than all the rest. I began to associate incarceration with pain. The food was painful, the beds, the lights, barbed-wired fences, the officers, the chairs, holidays away from family and friends, and the loss of focus to do something for humanity. Everything had become extremely painful for me. My mindset prior to my arrest would tell me: I can do this, it's nothing, I did it before. No wonder I would relapse so easily. There was not enough day to day association with pain. Many people can't see the pleasure in changing. When I began to make the changes, small changes, it had given me some positive momentum to continue on a positive path. My capacity to love grew stronger and stronger. My spirits came back to me. The kind of spirit a basketball player generates when they block a shot, get a steal, or score consecutive three pointers to bring their team back from a deficit. Suddenly the entire team catches this spiritual energy, even the fans. When people don't get help to face their painful memories, they become stuck with their emotional development. They cannot move forward until they have faced the past.

I suffered silently because I didn't keep it real. I didn't share my feeling of confusion, hurt and anger. When people tell you you'll be alright, man-up, or just forget about it, it will pass; I suggest you take immediate action. Don't just sit back and wish for it all to go away.

How? By changing your habits. Develop a list of values. Do you know how to get real smart; ask questions. I flunked out of being quiet. Too often we go around saying I can't change; this is who I am, it is in my blood. If you were told that you have only two days to live, what would you change in the world. We all have a SPECIAL GIFT of Free Will (Choice). The habits, rituals, and routines we all have were learned. I learned in prison that the tougher I got, the more the gangs wanted me to join them. As I said in earlier chapters, the majority of people in prison are not bad people. Ninety percent grew up with no real family life. Either their mom or dad died, or their mother had

126

multiple babies coming from several men. The mom and/or dad were likely alcoholics, drug users, or physical abusers who were themselves abused. They have seen close friends get killed by gunfire. For a child, these types of experiences greatly impact their emotional stability. These impacts went untreated. It isn't easy changing habits, but it can be done. BAD HABITS can take a variety of forms. Some of them you may not see as negative but they are; like drinking too much, over-reacting, controlling others, being perpetually late, or even always being in a hurry. As a child I developed some inappropriate sexual habits that were taught to me by other kids, I thank God that these negative habits did not last. Giving up, negative thinking, not talking about problems, complaining, hanging around people who caused trouble or got into trouble, procrastinating, these are all habits which happen to people who are angry or feel empty inside.

The first step to not being confused is to become aware that you have choices, and you see them by listing possibilities to a situation or circumstance that requires a decision. Then select the one that is the most meaningful to you. Reading may not be your problem; remembering is. So the solution is for you to practice repetition over and over. Thomas Edison tried 9,999 times to invent the light bulb. Someone asked him are you going to fail 10,000 times? Mr. Edison said, "I've never failed. I've learned 9,999 ways not to make a light bulb." My senior year in high school, I was confused. I was the number one hurdler and I saw no future. When I had a 1.65 grade point average, tutors and students helped me get it up to a 2.5 G.P.A. and graduation. I had to change. TODAY, demand more for yourself, I challenge you to believe you can do it! The most powerful source to help change human behavior is to Believe (Confidence). When you say I can do it, you gain power. Get an idea to help the world. Belief tells you what's possible and impossible. What we believe is the compass and map that guides us towards our goals.

I wore leg braces as a child and no one ever knew. No one ever knew that I would become an Olympic competitor either, but something powerful was in me. I loved running, and when you love something, you give both determination and persistence. If you get C's, D's or F's, all you can do is change your actions. Try a different way to study or try tutors. You do what you can do, then people will help you do what you can do. The only one that can predict your destiny or future is you! Being certain causes power. Roger Bannister (1954) was certain he could run the mile in under 4 minutes, now over 400 people have done it. The only way to create lasting change for yourself is to change the identity of who you really are. You're not a gangster, a bad person, a liar or a dummy. Everyone has potential.

Your ideas are important for America, and you are a solution to someone. Someone told me that if you can make someone smile or laugh, help cancer patients, feed the poor, or help old people, then you are a hero. I used to say I am a drug addict while trying to get better, now I say I'm a health nut. I motivate students; I'm a solution to someone. Don't say that I am a fat person; instead say that I am a healthy and athletic person. Change your identity. I used to think math was too hard. I'd say to myself, "I'm stupid." I changed my identity, to where I now say, "I'm smart." I just had to find another way to figure it out. Whenever something happens in your life the brain asks two questions: pain or pleasure? Change your attitude and think positive and your whole life will change. Thinking positive means you know that everything that happens to you will help in some way.

It is the small decisions that you and I make every day that create our destinies and make us heroes to others. Imagine if you worked in a hospital or a daycare. Suppose you were a fireman, a policeman, a lifeguard, or a counselor who helped criminals to change, an artist, a singer, dancer, doctor or a nurse. Any job that contributes to helping people will put you on a path to becoming a hero. So be funny, be crazy, have fun, take a chance, but the main thing is just learn from your mistakes in life. It's only a lesson, so don't try to be perfect. Find the reason for your problem, then get rid of it.

What are your life values? Values guide your destiny; anything that's important to you is a value. Your values are a belief system of what is right and wrong, or good and bad. Values are characteristics like commitment and determination. People who know and live by their values become leaders in our society. Leaders include anyone able to impact the lives of another person like teachers, business owners, news reporters, firefighters, pilots, etc. Once you know what's most important to you, making a decision to do it is easy. Most people who overdo it, don't know which things are most important in their life. Getting a buzz became important to me and that buzz stopped me from achieving. The direction of your life will be controlled by your values. There was this woman who studied the effect of training animals with pain. It worked for the most part until she tried to apply pain on a dolphin and it swam away. This caused her to ease up and try positive reinforcement. Lives are controlled by pain and pleasure, always wanting to have a good time. Unfortunately, most of the pleasure comes from partying. If you are feeling bad, mad, or bored, let's party! It can lead to alcohol and substance abuse. I want you to put intelligence first, to evaluate your situation. Weigh things out.

Discern what the consequences are, and make intelligence a high priority. Earning better grades, working in a field you enjoy, and having love in your life will give you a natural high on life, which is much better than drugs or alcohol.

I once worked in the field of special education and found out that no one is smarter than anyone else. Some of us just require a different strategy or a different way to learn the same things. You have to accept responsibility for your actions and stop blaming others. Say, "It happened because of a choice I made" and then you'll start evaluating your choices and making more intelligent ones.

Your past does not equal your future. Once you accept responsibility, you are no longer pushed by what you have to be, ought to be, or what you must do. You can do what you want to do. People get hooked on drugs, overeating, smoking etc., because they like the experience and don't know any other way to get the same state of mind that feels that good.

I want you to think about a time you really enjoyed something you liked. From now on, use that same thought for everything. Accepting responsibility means that if someone does you wrong, very wrong, the person who did it did not make you feel angry. They are not responsible for making you feel that way. The anger was a response you created from being wronged. You have the power and choice to feel differently. People don' have the power over you, you choose. You already have the power; if you don't feel like you have the power that's because you don't have God's inspiration in you.

EFFORT + QUESTIONS = SUCCESS

At the end of my junior year at Kansas State, I received a dismissal notice for failing to meet academic requirements to sustain my eligibility in order to retain my athletic scholarship. The reality had hit me hard. Why couldn't I see the funnel cloud forming before the tornado hit me. It was because my priorities were screwed-up. I had placed more emphasis on partying at the clubs and ended up spending less time studying, when it should have been the opposite. Intelligence should have been first.

That summer, I worked really hard and regained my academic standing, which made me eligible to participate. I sweated that one out. When the chips were down, I responded in a positive way. I buckled down and cut out the things that were holding me back from succeeding in both the classroom and on the field of athletics. You should never forget that you are a student first. If you remember that, then if everything that relates to you athletically begins to go wrong like an injury or

134

frustration with other players or the coaches, or the attention promised you before you signed the letter of intent never happened, then as long as your priorities are in their proper order, you won. If your focus is not on academics but on sports, then when things start going wrong, it will have a negative emotional impact on you.

Many potentially great students and athlete have given up on their hopes and dreams. Many have quit school and lived a life of *"If I could of, I would of and I should of."* My academic counselors Professor Henry Camp and Berry Surtec Sr., advised me during my fall, and gave me an insight to the true value of my priorities and how they relate to my life. They showed me a way out when I couldn't see any open windows. I listened to them intently, and their honesty and concern allowed me to open-up, pay attention and take action. I followed their advice step by step. If you are open and totally honest about the things that bother you while speaking to your counselors, I guarantee they will be able to guide you through it, giving you a new and clear vision.

By the time the summer ended, I had made it! It was the first time in my life that I had earned A's and B's. Everything I had ever gotten or learned was because I kept an open mind for suggestions and advice. Then my Academic Counselors allowed others to guide me through this journey. The new change created a new fire inside of me. I was filled with confidence. Everything I did or tried from that day forward was achieved without fear. Efforts and questions were the key to my understanding and comprehension. My athletic career really took off with this new fire: the realization that I can do anything I put my mind to. I quickly excelled among the ranks of several former Olympians and medalists from gold to bronze. I adopted the warm-up stretching routine from watching four-time Olympic gold medalist Carl Lewis. I learned to train every day and not take a day off from my trainer Steve Miller, because that's what Edwin Moses did. I roomed with Olympic medalist Al Joyner. I ran a photo finish at the 1984 Drake Relays in Iowa and witnessed the famous 100 meter race of Carl Lewis and the

NFL's best running-back, Herschel Walker of the Dallas Cowboys.

Herschel Walker was a senior from the University of Georgia who was 6'2" and weighed about 240 lbs. Herschel had lighting speed and he ran neck-and-neck with Carl, only to be edged out by Lewis at the tape.

A teammate of mine, Doug Lytle, made the team in the Pole-Vault event in 1984 and placed sixth. On August 16th, 2010, a Jamaican Olympian sprinter named Usain Bolt, ran a 9.58 world record run in the 100 meters. He trained hard, but most of all, he believed in himself. Mr. Usain Bolt also broke the world record in the 200-meter dash with 19.16 seconds in August, 2009 at the famous Berlin Olympic Stadium in Germany. He trained hard and most of all, he believed in himself.

In 2001, I had the exciting pleasure of running into Channel 7 ABC Sports Reporter, Jim Rose, while shopping at a grocery store in Matteson, Illinois. I talked to him briefly about my relationship with Craig Hodges (Chicago Bulls legendary basketball player), with reference to helping youth and my desire to recommit to helping youth who often suffer from depression. Mr. Rose surprised me. He's a real down to earth person who cares about others.

One morning while incarcerated, I was in the middle of writing a song for my UP L.I.F.T. Project when the Oprah Winfrey Show came on television with a special guest, Halle Berry, who spoke of her weakness – "being attracted to love." As I listened to her give insight after her time of healing from a broken relationship, she said to Oprah, "I remember that you told me long ago that without integrity, there's no Love." I immediately thought, "That's how my Father and Mother, Family and friend's relationships grew stronger." My thoughts about relationships were forever changed.

STAYING FOCUSED

I come from a family of good athletes. All of my brothers excelled in track. As a teenager, I grew up with a great group of friends who were also excellent athletes. Many have gone on to become professional athletes as well as teachers and coaches at high schools. We all excelled because of our ability to remain focused, even through tough times. Staying focused is critical for anyone doing just about anything from the largest to the simplest task.

A high school teammate and friend, Craig Hodges, former NBA Champion, would never leave a Chicago Bulls practice until he had made 150 three pointers. This habit brought forth an automatic response to hit his target with great accuracy. If there ever was a person that had an exceptional work ethic in the basketball arena, it was Craig Hodges.

I watched, played and practiced with him for years before he became an NBA star. His discipline and determination was second to none. I recall a conversation he had with my dad.

Craig came to pick me up to go and play some ball and then hang out for a while. My dad and I were watching the Chicago Cubs play the Pittsburg Pirates. Yeah, I am one of those die-hard Cub fans, but my dad cheered for any team that played against the Cubs. He was a Chicago White Sox fan, so you know we used to go at it. Dad stood up with great admiration and ultimate respect, tipping his hat to Craig's accomplishments. He remembered hearing about Craig's talent when Craig was only sixteen years old. He said to Craig, "Congratulations, but just be careful to keep your religious beliefs separate from your business, because if you don't, those people will make trouble for you." Who those people were I did not know, but my dad seemed to know. While we were leaving the house, Craig asked me, "Why does your dad always put me on the hot seat?" I responded, "I know man, you know how my father is."

One year later, my father passed away and it turned out that his wisdom to all of my family members and friends had come to pass. Craig took a stand to draw awareness to the plight of the poor communities in the United States by presenting a letter to the President of the United States, Mr. George H.W. Bush, expressing his concern; and ever since that day, Craig never saw the NBA again. Sources around the league allegedly spread the word that Craig was a troublemaker.

He was one of the greatest pure long distance shooters in the history of the NBA, Craig and Larry Bird are on a podium sitting alone at the top to this very day. His records include: most three-point field goals made in a half (5); the most three-point field goals made in a quarter (5); the most consecutive three point goals made (9); the highest free throw percentage as of 2010' (.900); the winner of three consecutive All Star game long distance shootouts. He twice led the league in three-point accuracy and helped the Chicago Bulls in his final two seasons (1990-92). He played three seasons with the Milwaukee Bucks and averaged double figures, setting an NBA record with (.491) behind the arc with 86 out of 175. Hodges was a spot player on Chicago's first two championship teams, retiring with a career average of (8.5) in (695-games) and a

(.400) career three-point average. He has spent a lot of time raising money for underprivileged inner-city schools. His career spans over twelve seasons, including playing for the Clippers and Phoenix Suns. At the age of 32, Craig was reluctantly forced to retire and then began his coaching career. I can only imagine what thoughts were going through his mind as he was coaching, knowing that he was still a much better player than his teammates.

This new fire to live and change the direction in my life now requires me to stay focused on a daily basis to avoid skidding back to a point of no return. There are going to still be some ups and downs, good times and bad, fast and slow. However, if the focus remains, then progress will eventually shine.

In 2004 at the age of forty-four, I had a corrective knee surgery to repair damaged bone tissue from an injury that occurred 20 years earlier back in 1984. This knee injury, which ended my track career, was originally from a child born deformity, but had escalated several weeks prior to the 1984 Olympic trials.

I was sitting in a good position, climbing up the ladder of the ranks at number six in the United States. I was picked as an outside shot to make the team according to all of the track and field polls. However, they were unaware of my injury. I kept it a secret and no matter how much I tried to focus on the race, all I could think about was the pain. Unable to advance, my vision had dispersed. Years later, following the knee surgery, the doctors informed me that if I rehabilitated the knee correctly, I would be able to run and jump not only as fast and as high as before, but even higher than ever. I lifted weights to strengthen my upper body and legs, then picked-up a basketball, all at age 47, and exploded off the ground to a sounding dunk. I'm once again enjoying basketball and today I play with people in their 20s and 30s.

To believe is the most powerful force in humanity. Anthony Robbins showed me a unique and quick way to move forward from negative obstacles that hindered my well-being. In fact, I remember verbatim just about everything that I studied under him, and now I am fortunate to deliver my message in a more practical way.

I recommend to anyone that may be struggling with their emotions, finances, relationships, substance abuse or homelessness, to look for any self-help book that has a positive impact on the author's life. I learned to adopt beliefs that work for other people. There's always a way to do better in every aspect of my life, as long as I don't quit trying. My entire life changed from park benches to Park Avenue, from jail to feeling swell. Faith will ignite the fire.

For the future, this new Fire will drive you to a new happiness, and things that you put off will be back on your menu. Things you forgot will come back to you. You will see a new vision and have a much better focus. You will gain a new confidence. This new fire begins when you say, "I'm no longer going to live this way; I deserve better and I will do better."

This NEW FIRE! begins when you tell yourself, "I'm not going to quit." This new fire is called Desire. The new fire begins when you say, "I'm not taking it anymore, and from now on I'm going to start treating myself better." When you say these things to yourself, you automatically raise your standards to a higher level; your self-esteem will amazingly begin to change. This new Fire! begins today.

Depression had brought me to an all-time low; it had me fill out applications to get permanent disability. I met this guy who drank so much that he crashed into a pole at 85 mph and survived. There was another who overdosed three times and spent seven months in a coma, but is now living a normal life. Another guy was shot two times, and on the way to the hospital, he asked the driver to stop and get him some heroin. Their problems were all created by anger and by not having good direction and appropriate coping skills to get beyond the obstacles. I once thought that when I turned 40, I wouldn't be able to play basketball as well as I could in my younger years, and now at 47-48 years old, I am still dunking the ball. It is all because I set a new goal and commitment to practice, jogging, and strengthening the areas that would increase my ability. I began to do explosive training movements.

The Power in you is much greater than the power that's holding you back. You've got to focus on what's right and not what's wrong. You have to keep on setting goals. Don't put it off any longer, start making changes now!

My former track coaches at Kansas State in the mid-80s, John Capriotti, Gregg Kraft, McVey and Randy Cole, have all been successful and are presently enjoying the fruits of their labored success. They were a part of my village and circumference that helped shape my confidence and character as a student-athlete. They also have a great sense of humor. One particular day, the head coach, Steve Miller, suggested that we could work on my weakness or we can build on my strengths, with reference to training in my senior year in track and making a run to qualify for the Olympic Team. We decided to focus on my strengths. He then put me with the middle distance runners for a two month training period. We ran repeat 800, 8-10 of them over hilly gravel surfaces, while Randy Cole helped increase my mileage run from 2.5 to 6 miles. I would have never, ever believed that I could have jogged 6 miles, but the coaches were skilled at teaching the athletes the methods of training, how will we benefit and then map out the steps, objectives and ultimate goal. They never put the emphasis on winning. Instead, the emphasis was on competing and the possibilities would take care of themselves. Today, Gregg Kraft is one of the 2008 Division I, Track and Field Champion Coaches, and Coach Capriotti is an excellent coach and influential in the world-wide marketing of Track and Field.

The point I am making is that the success in coaching and in these peoples' lives were a strength to me. For example; when Steve Miller surrounded himself with intelligent, positive, and open-minded people who committed themselves to character building blocks of success like desire, effort, stick-to-itiveness, good attitude, and the willingness to study and learn; they created a village network of support within the Kansas State University confines, and this village rubbed-off on anyone who bought into their philosophy. If you had even an iota of potential, then they were sure to bring it out of you. Staying focused is what usually separates those who are able to perform in competition at maximum levels, even as the pressure heightens, from those who never make it. Remember to set goals, because goals give you direction. If you ever find yourself drifting away from your goals due to life's circumstance, which at times can cause a change in your course; by having goals you'll be able to re-connect the dots that will lead you back to your focus. There have been lots of people who had or have projects that have been put on the back burner for years, and they ended up living a life of regret. We don't have to live a life of regrets, so "GO For It!" and see what the unforeseen in your life has for you.

I'm sure many of my poor decisions angered Coach Miller and filled him with disappointment. However, He never judged me. He drew out the potential in me by still believing in me. His belief helped me to believe stronger and focus on using my time, talent and gifts to help others. This was the tipping point for me, and I have been focused and on fire to leave a legacy of "helping others" ever since.

I wrote this book 3 ½ years before it was printed, thanks to a conversation with my former coach, Steve Miller, which re-lit the fire in my life to get beyond the past wreckage of my life. Because I was willing to reach out to others, I realized I do not need to remain a victim, and can go on to once again succeed in my endeavors.

I know how difficult the teenage years can be. You are no longer a child, but you are not quite an adult yet. Your body is changing physically and it may seem like you don't fit in or belong anywhere Rest assured that you are precious and can go on to accomplish great things, despite the many obstacles that may be in your path. You are blessed to live in a country, even with all of its faults, that has tremendous resources of every kind to help you overcome and be a success. Don't succumb to pressure that education is a bad thing; it is the key to breaking out of the cycle of poverty, confusion and depression you may find yourself in. Go for it, and remember "It's on u."

90294652R00092

Made in the USA
Lexington, KY
09 June 2018